A Practical Guide to Educating *for* Responsibility in Management and Business

A Practical Guide to Educating *for* Responsibility in Management and Business

Ross McDonald

businessexpert
Press

A Practical Guide to Educating for Responsibility in Management and Business
Copyright © Business Expert Press, LLC, 2013.

First published in 2013 by
Business Expert Press, LLC
222 East 46th Street, New York, NY 10017
www.businessexpertpress.com

ISBN-13: 978-1-60649-714-2 (paperback)
ISBN-13: 978-1-60649-715-9 (e-book)

Business Expert Press Principles of Responsible
Management Education (PRME) collection

Collection ISSN: Forthcoming (print)
Collection ISSN: Forthcoming (electronic)

Cover and interior design by Exeter Premedia Services Private Ltd.
Chennai, India

First edition: 2013

10 9 8 7 6 5 4 3 2 1

Printed in the United States of America.

Abstract

Educating *for* Responsibility is a new way of engaging young people with the challenge of changing their world for the better. Designed for application in any educational context dealing with ethics, responsibility, or human development it bases classroom practice on facilitating an expanding ability to think and act in more fully responsible ways. In contrast to the predominant model of teaching which is almost exclusively an intellectual education *about* responsibility, educating *for* responsibility integrates emotion, insight, observation and action in a whole person learning much more fitting with the true dynamics of exercising this resilient capacity. In this short volume, the need for rapid change in how we educate for responsibility is explained and a template offered for a creative way of teaching that has proven to be extremely effective in practice. Written particularly for those offering courses or training in social responsibility, sustainability or business ethics it offers a new way of thinking about how we might better serve the interests of a generation of young people entering a rapidly changing, and by all accounts, rapidly destabilising world. In these pages, an internationally recognized teacher, shares the results of thirty years of educational experimentation aimed at helping students become part of building a better world. In educating *for* responsibility the classroom becomes a place for collaboration, integration and reflection—and a laboratory for actualizing our individual and collective potentials for truly responsible being in the world.

Keywords

responsibility, values education, business ethics, CSR, sustainable business, business strategy, future studies, whole person learning, humanistic education.

Contents

CHAPTER 1

Education *for* Responsibility—What It Is and Why It Is Important

- The Importance of Educating *for* Responsibility
- The Meaning of Responsibility
- The Problems of Education as Usual
- The Principles of Changing Practice
  - Open and Friendly Learning Spaces
  - Challenging Questions
  - Constant Discussion

Education is the most powerful weapon you can use to change the world.

Nelson Mandela

If education is always to be conceived along the same antiquated lines of a mere transmission of knowledge there is little to be hoped from it in the bettering of man's future. For what is the use of transmitting knowledge if the individual's total development lags behind?

Maria Montessori

The Importance of Teaching *for* Responsibility

This short book is written for teachers working to bring forth a greater responsibility in the world. It will be particularly relevant to those working in the related areas of business ethics, social responsibility, and sustainability as the approaches discussed have been developed specifically with these areas in mind. But here, there will also be much of help to others working with other groups. The techniques described in the following pages under the banner of "educating *for* responsibility" are general ones and can find wide application, given that they are designed as pedagogical practices through which the critical content is developed by the learners themselves. The approach can, and has been, applied across subject and cultural boundaries to considerable effect and its flexibility allows it to be used in a variety of contexts limited only by one's imagination and creativity. It can easily be adapted for use with younger children and older professionals and well might be, as responsibility is a capacity relevant to all ages, cultures, and times. The particular focus here though is young adults, specifically learners in their late teens and twenties studying at undergraduate level.

As things stand, there is little available in the way of genuinely practical advice for those teachers who aspire to improve their effectiveness in this important domain and there is a real need to begin sharing more of what works and what doesn't work in the classroom. In the main, it would be fair to say that most teachers (and university ones in particular) get few opportunities for formal teacher training in areas related to responsibility and are left to feel their way toward successful practice. Yet given the mounting challenges we now face as a global society, we would be well-advised to begin bringing a more focused approach to bear if our work is to really impact the future positively.

For the past 30 years I have been actively experimenting with a wide range of alternative approaches in a search to find the most effective way of building a resilient capacity for responsibility in the classroom. For necessary reasons that will be explained in the following pages, this search has taken me far from the standard teaching model. The results have been astonishing and deeply humbling leading not only to literally thousands of very satisfied students, but also to a range of institutional, national, and international awards for effectiveness in teaching. I cannot claim that the model as it now stands is in any way perfect but I do know that it is a considerable improvement on "education as usual." Hopefully it offers others the opportunity to think in new and much more creative ways about what we are trying to achieve and how we might do it more effectively.

Although I was trained as a psychologist, I have devoted my professional life to working in business schools as these are such critically important places for determining the quality of our collective future. There can be little doubt that business is one of the forces most powerfully shaping the direction of the contemporary world and although it brings huge and varied benefit, it is also deeply problematic as a singular ordering philosophy. Almost every report on the declining state of the world—failing climate stability, falling food supplies, crashing biodiversity, and disappearing resources—identifies "business as usual" as the key factor in compounding our problems. This rather loose term refers to a whole cultivated social system based on maximizing economic growth, and as this now pushes against the limits of a closed natural system, the need to change our fundamental thinking about the place of business in a responsible order increases by the day. Sitting at the heart of this process, business schools occupy a unique space and harbor a unique potential to foster positive change.

It is particularly important that those of us on the front line apply ourselves to this work seriously and soon given the various crises that are currently unfolding will play themselves out in the lifetimes of the young people we teach. Top-level scientific reports on climate change, food security, fish stocks, ecological integrity, and regional conflict point to the next 10 to 30 years as being a critical window of opportunity for change. In each of these areas the indices of thriving are currently declining, creating dismal projections for young peoples' futures. Yet as the famous Chinese ideogram has it, every crisis is also an opportunity and this generation of students is *the* generation that has the greatest (and perhaps even final) chance to usher in a more responsible order while there is still time. As educators it is our duty to help empower young people to build a better future for themselves, and primary in that preparation is an enhancement in the capacity for responsible action. All indications are that if we fail in our obligations to this generation, we will fail every generation that follows. Working to facilitate more responsibility among this generation of future business leaders is then crucial work at a critical time.

Yet, the gravity of our own responsibilities as teachers in these realms is not yet being taken as seriously as it ought to be. It is true that business schools worldwide are increasingly embedding courses in responsibility, ethics, and sustainability into their permanent degree structures and in some cases even requiring that students take these to graduate. These are encouraging trends yet many, if not most, of these courses are delivered in ways that unwittingly compromise any real potential to facilitate practical change. At root, most involve learning only *about* responsibility in abstract intellectual terms. We give theories, case studies, and assessments all emphasizing what distant others think responsibility entails and while this is intellectually interesting, it generally fails to involve learners in exploring their own capacities for action in the context of their own lives. As an education *for* responsibility, it is a remarkably limited approach and much of its lack of vision stems from an insufficient appreciation of what responsibility actually requires if it is to flourish.

The Meaning of Responsibility

What then is this thing called responsibility? In broad use, the term signifies an ability to be broadly considerate and to extend boundaries of consideration to include the interests of others. In this sense it is an inherently ethical notion, one that recognizes the tension between personal and collective benefit. To be unethical, or immoral, or irresponsible is to think, speak, and act in ways that unduly benefit the self, or the few, at the expense of often numerous others. Ethical, moral, and spiritual systems accordingly argue for the transcendence of narrow self-concern and the emergence of a way of being that recognizes others as being of equal importance to ourselves. This is the essential end sought by Utilitarianism, Kantian thought, Christianity, Buddhism, and the Corporate Social Responsibility movement among many others. In each of these schools of thought, responsibility—ethical responsiveness in other words, is understood to be a maturing potential, one to be cultivated to ensure our thriving. Accordingly, the vast majority of the world's ethical writings aim to justify and encourage more considerate behavior and offer practical methods for moving beyond the narrowly considered conduct that forces suffering upon others.

With this in mind, the working definition that I find most useful in practice sees responsibility as *an emergent ability to skillfully respond to the demands of the world in ways that facilitate a maximally harmonious thriving.* There are several aspects of this working definition that deserve attention. First, in seeing responsibility as literally the *ability* to respond, its nature as a capacity or a skill is made more apparent. To be responsible is to integrate a variety of capabilities simultaneously, including the ability to listen and learn, to compromise, negotiate, reflect, empathize, and engage self-restraint. It requires attention, intelligence and emotional maturity among other capacities and is accordingly a multidimensional and holistic accomplishment. To assume responsibility is also to seek an alignment or a fundamental *harmony* of interests across constituencies such that conflict, oppression, and suffering are minimized in the whole. Embedded in this is an understanding of responsibility as an *expanding* potential that can be applied to extend care across broad domains. We all have a strong sense of responsibility for our own thriving and we tend to ensure that our personal needs are well catered to. In most cases, and as a general matter of course, we also extend our sense of responsibility to include the well-being of those we are closely connected to—friends and family in particular. Within these twin domains, we work to ensure a harmony of outcomes and a mutual thriving for all. Many also actively extend boundaries of consideration beyond this to include the well-being of the community and society they live in. People willingly pay taxes, vote, participate in fund-raising events, give to charity, and volunteer their time to benefit others. And some extend responsibility even farther, to work for the benefit of even more distant constituencies—coming generations and threatened ecosystems being only two examples. Responsibility is then an *emergent* potential and its actualization involves a constant transcendence of limiting, largely unconscious boundaries. These boundaries constrain our understanding and create inevitable conflict when the perceived needs of self, family, society and nature come to contradict each other.

The conflicts caused by a limited sense of responsibility are at root a function of what we *care* about and what we fail to care about. If I care only for myself, then sooner rather than later, I will cause friction and irritation to community, friends, and family as I fail to give due consideration to their coexisting needs. Similarly, if we think only of our own tribal, cultural, class, or gender interests, we will run into conflict with those lying outside these limited boundaries. And critically in these times, if we think only of our own generation's needs, we will build a fundamental conflict with the interests of all those who will inherit the mounting problems our self-indulgence will create. In all of these, conflict and suffering are the result of limiting our expressions of care. The drive to develop a more extensive responsibility seeks to reduce painful conflict and find *harmony* among the interests of otherwise competing constituencies. It is then a development driven by expanding boundaries of inclusive *care*.

As things stand, we are clearly failing to care enough. Hundreds of millions of people in the world go to bed hungry each night and have no access to clean water or meaningful medical care. In the natural world, thousands of species are disappearing at an unprecedented rate as ecosystems are "developed" and destroyed and the balance of critical systems, like the Arctic, forced into a literal meltdown. The consequences of this for future generations are largely ignored as we continue to seek the narrowly extended and short-lived benefits of business as usual. The root problem is that if we don't care for distant others or for future generations, we will feel no need to act responsibly toward them.

To develop our potential for a more responsible mode of being in the world we need to come to care about what is happening to it—both now and as we look forward. As a complex development, responsibility involves much more than instilling an intellectual understanding *about* responsibility. It demands an integrated expansion of our intellectual, emotional, and motivational capacities in a harmonious improvement that enables more caring and responsible action. Such well-rounded development is hindered rather than helped by much of what we currently do in the name of education and in seeing what responsibility entails more definitively, we can work to remove some of the major roadblocks that education as usual puts in the way of educating *for* responsibility.

The Problems of Education As Usual

Much of our current approach to teaching about responsibility is based on limited reflection as to how responsibility develops and a critical failure to fully appreciate its dynamic qualities. As indicated above, responsibility is an *emergent* potential—one that works by continuously expanding and transcending limiting boundaries. The potential for a broader responsibility is endless and the world is full of examples of people acting with great skill to ensure the thriving of multitudes of their fellows. To fully appreciate responsibility is to see it as an unfolding potential that comes from *within* the person and, as such, to see the role of teaching *for* responsibility as working to bring this potential out into a fuller expression. Yet this dynamic runs counter to the vast preponderance of contemporary teaching practice which aims instead to force into the learner a purely external understanding—the impersonal theories, studies, articles, and data that define any academic discipline. In this approach, developing personal perspective is frustrated as information and insight flows in a single direction—from teacher to learner. In such a dynamic, open expression and active questioning are stifled and the potential to bring forth an emergent sense of responsibility is frustrated. Why this is so deserves some deeper consideration.

In my own extensive explorations as a teacher I have come to view the standard model of education as deeply suboptimal when it is applied to teaching for more sustainable, ethical, and responsible conduct. The problems are many, but all stem from the basic belief that responsible capacity must somehow be developed from the outside rather than from the inside. Our classrooms are accordingly structured to maximally facilitate the transfer of external perspective into the learner's mind. Classes are arranged for large groups in which a single teacher provides authoritative facts about an area of study—ones to be ingested, retained, and reproduced in a series of individualized assessments. Courses are planned around rigid curricula and class time devoted by and large to note-giving, note-taking, and video-watching. Such a format is the default option in much of higher education and classes of this form dominate most disciplines and in some cases this is of course appropriate. When teaching basic, non-contentious facts and skills, it may be a workable model; but its application as a standardized mode of teaching has become so universal that it is too often unthinkingly adopted as the only legitimate approach. In truth though, there are other ways of working and many that are far more suited to developing a responsible potential.

From the point of view of educating *for* responsibility, the standard model is deeply problematic in that it negates the value of students' own views and denies them participation in cultivating an expanding responsibility for themselves. The dismissal of potential implicit in this is patronizing and wholly underestimates the drive for improvement inherent in the young people we teach. Few, if any, wish to cause suffering for others and most are highly motivated to connect with and care about the world around them. There is a deep-seated desire to discuss and explore questions of responsibility as a basic human concern but all too often this is quashed by education as usual. In many cases it is quashed from the outset by arranging learning in large classes of a hundred or more people—spaces where there is very little chance that students will feel comfortable speaking their minds. We all feel self-conscious when speaking in large groups of strangers and young people are particularly sensitive to the judgments of their peers. It is then, only in the rarest of large classes, that conversations involving large numbers of learners are possible. The model of mass knowledge transfer that defines most tertiary teaching may be efficient, but it demands an extraordinary passivity on the part of learners.

Meaningful involvement is also reduced by the sheer rigidity of most courses where every meeting is preplanned for delivering a particular topic. This leaves no opportunity to stop and debate confusions as they arise, or to explore contrary viewpoints, or to probe more deeply into underlying assumptions as we are all constantly having to "move on" to "keep to schedule." Students in large, rigidly-structured classes typically learn early on that there is little point to interjection as their questions are given short-shrift or sacrificed to the transcendent needs of the timetable. The result is a silenced passivity and a repression of emergent voice and perspective.

A third element of the dominant model that blocks the emergence of a responsible capability is the degree to which the subject is dealt with in an overwhelmingly rational and abstract way. Academics tend to gravitate naturally towards high intellectualism as a matter of course, and most learning experiences consequently involve heavy doses of the latest literature drawn from the most scholarly journals. While these materials may contain important insights, they rarely resonate with students who typically find the tone and style of academic writing seriously off-putting. (This is observable in the fact that considerable force commonly has to be applied to ensure that people "do the readings.") In large part, the inability of students to relate whole-heartedly to the "literature" stems from its dryness and obscurity. Academic writing is of a peculiarly non-literary form—a fact most evidenced by its stringent demand that all uncertainty, emotion, and subjective preference be minimized. As a result, it is rarely moving and in excluding all emotional reference, it renders itself hard to care about for most students. The high abstraction is rarely felt as being relevant to their own lives as emotional, intuitive and subjective people. When unrelenting, the constant presentation of academic theory serves to further pacify learners as they are encouraged to engage only on an intellectual plane with abstract concepts that they do not really care about, or easily relate to.

Another key failing of the dominant model is the dynamic of fear that is required to obtain its objectives, a fear that particularly surrounds assessment. Learning in the modern academy is pushed rather than pulled as learners are forced into a divisive environment characterized by authority and competition. Good grades are limited and all know that there will inevitably be winners and losers. The fear of being labeled a failure is very real and a constant stress for students. This fear encourages conformity and submissiveness, and a further retraction from expanding a tentative capacity. Far too many classes in all subject areas reduce learning to study for "what is on the exam" as all learning beyond that limit attenuates. Inbuilt competition also undoes one of the most powerfully positive dynamics we have available to us—that of actively cooperative learning.

When we place people in a competitive environment we create insecurity and force them to attend to their own interests first and to frame these as oppositional to the interests of others. This leads to a host of suboptimal behaviors including the common tendencies to co-opt the most essential resources for assignments and withhold critical insights for fear of losing advantage in the competitive grading stakes. Assessment is defined in wholly individualized terms and meaningful collaboration on examined work is usually threatened with dire punishment. Among other things, the end result is a repression of responsible action as learners leave their peers to struggle in confusion and offer no assistance to help the whole advance. All of this adds critically to a learning culture dominated by isolation, anxiety, and an uncritical passivity.

Fear, isolation, disengagement, and passivity are the inevitable consequence of education as usual and they are all obstructive to the emergence of a meaningfully constructed sense of personal responsibility. As a complex, unfolding potential, responsibility seeks to harmonize the personal

interest with the collective one and young people are particularly interested in balancing these imperatives as they enter into the adult world.
They also have a strong desire to learn from their peers and develop their
own authoritative voice. Yet most of the structuring of education as usual
serves to frustrate these natural desires. If we are to progress towards a
more meaningful and fitting mode of education we need to remove these
structural barriers and begin to work more fully *with* the dynamics of
unfolding responsibility, and not against them. We need to begin treating
the young people we teach with more respect and recognize their inherent
desire to become more fully responsible. The "banking" approach to
learning can be a deeply dysfunctional one that most apply unthinkingly
simply because it is the norm. If we are to more effectively empower this
generation of young people to build a better future for themselves, we
need to think well beyond the limitations outlined and engage a mode
that is in many ways its polar opposite.

The Principles of Changing Practice

The starting point for change is the clear recognition of how badly the
current model of teaching goes against the natural grain of an emerging
responsibility. In the real world, we typically resolve the many moral conflicts we encounter by discussing them with others around us and by
bringing a broad range of factors to bear including personal experience,
emotion, and intuition. As we banish each of these from the classroom we
dismember the capacity for a well-rounded and realistic responsibility and
work against its resilient cultivation. The hopeful assumption seems to be
that the intellectual authority of experts will be powerful enough in itself
to shift personal behavior long into the future. Yet this fails to appreciate
that in all probability, the young people we teach will not resolve any
future dilemmas by re-reading Aristotle or recalling the details of a case
study on corporate fraud. They will instead act according to what they
themselves feel is the best course of action at that moment. If we genuinely
want to improve the likelihood of responsible action we need to start dealing more directly with what is *in the minds of the people we teach in the
present* rather than what has been on the minds of distant others in the
past. The ultimate aim of education is to improve personal conduct and

this begins with improving thinking. This is made much more likely when how and what learners are thinking is made visible and worked with as the primary material of interest.

Given the inherent subjectivity of responsible judgment and the fact that people make decisions according to their own perspective, to get the values, confusions, barriers, habits, assumptions, half-truths, and hopes of learners into the open is to bring into play the key dynamics that actively facilitate or debilitate individual responsibility. In working with what students themselves think, barriers can be challenged, personal hunches tested, and contradictions resolved. The result is a much more nuanced approach tailored to directly addressing the unique dynamics of any particular group of learners. In dealing directly with their *own* views of their *own* responsibilities in the context of their *own* lives, learning becomes maximally engaging, relevant, and empowering. Working with learners' existing understandings is then the key to educating *for* responsibility and to bring this out effectively, three essential structural dynamics need to be in place. These are open and friendly spaces, challenging questions, and constant discussion. By basing learning on these three principles, the restrictions of conventional teaching are largely transcended and the whole operative energy of the classroom transformed.

Open and Friendly Learning Spaces

Learning *for* responsibility puts teaching practice closer to the original meaning of the term "education" which rightfully translated means "to bring forth from within." The process seeks to work directly with students thinking in order to remove barriers, undo confusions, and make learning maximally resonant. This requires that students feel free enough to speak their minds, share their feelings, and voice uncertainty, doubt and disagreement. This is possible only when there is a friendly and receptive atmosphere in which respect reigns.

The most essential prerequisite for successfully building an open and friendly learning space is a relatively small class size. I have experimented with classes of all sizes over the years and I know that in large groups, it is practically impossible to create the levels of intimacy necessary for deep personal learning. The sheer anonymity of large classes renders them impersonal and unwelcoming places for self-revelation. An ideal group for this form of learning is between 20 and 50 students. This brings together a sufficient diversity of perspective in a still manageable group dynamic. Assuming that one can arrange such a functional class size there are a number of further means for creating a sense of safety and openness that are very useful in practice. These involve building healthy working relationships between teacher and learners, and between the learners themselves.

Cultivating Harmonious Relationships Between Teacher and Learners

To work with students in the way educating *for* responsibility demands is to minimize the formal power difference between teacher and learner. In most classes teachers retain an often overbearing power to judge, down-grade, fail, or otherwise punish the uninspired. Poorly wielded authority dehumanizes learning and makes learners fearful and closed. To facilitate emergent learning, students must feel free to question and critique what the teacher is arguing. It is imperative then that from the outset, we establish that it is the *authority of ideas* that is most important and that a constant questioning of what is being said is essential for real learning to occur. This code has to be sincere though, as students will quickly see through any displays of contradictory defensiveness or authoritarianism. To work with learners respectfully requires a genuine openness to challenge and an ability to admit not knowing or being mistaken. These are often dreaded states for teachers employing a knowledge transfer model of teaching and much of the formal authority we shelter behind seeks to repress these possibilities.

Yet there is nothing really to fear. In fact it is fair to say that when we as teachers find ourselves not having all the answers, or any answers or the wrong answers, we find ourselves in a highly constructive space. New questions come as we reach the limits of what we know and pursuing them *with* students gives the opportunity for all to see further. If this spirit can be honestly conveyed to a class, it creates a comfortable and respectful environment into which both vigorous and tentative expression can come. We ask our students to recognize their limitations and to be open to new learning and considerable traction is gained if the teacher models this spirit. It sets a constructive tone of mutual enquiry in which the teacher and the learners find themselves in a common search for better understanding. Anyway, admitting to not having all the answers garners much more respect that the clumsy buffoonery that often accompanies our transparently inept stabs in the dark.

The formal authority of the teacher is typically maximized around the lightning rod of assessed work and this needs to be approached with a particular sensitivity. The question of how one can assess in an emergent learning framework is covered in Chapter Four of this writing, but it is important at this point to make a few comments about how the most paralyzing anxieties around assessment can be tempered. First, it is essential to note that the common practice of giving final examinations is of a strictly limited utility as these can only really deal with the narrow intellectual aspects of learning. It is generally preferable to have learners concern themselves with things other than taking perfect notes and not having a final examination comes as a huge relief as all can then focus on being more fully present in the classroom. A more constructive use of assessment is to internally arrange it around exercises that involve practicing more responsible thought and action.

However the assessment is done, it is important to create as cooperative an environment as possible to ease sharing. Competition should be minimized by making good grades available to all who perform at a high standard and cooperation can help as many to this outcome as possible. Expressive work can be assessed not by any preset grade distribution or singular model answer but by the extent to which it exhibits an expanding ability to integrate understanding into more farsighted, broadminded, deeply considered, and ultimately responsible perspectives. Anxiety can be allayed by ensuring that all assignment questions are debated and fine-tuned by the learners themselves to ensure their relevance and usefulness. Furthermore, sharing answers, allowing failing assignments to be redone, and giving extensive and targeted feedback ensures that every opportunity is given to assist students in achieving success. There are many ways to make students feel safe to challenge and express their thinking but underlying them all is a fundamental respect and helpfulness from the teacher that refuses to threaten or patronize.

Cultivating Harmonious Relationships Between Students

If the most common barriers to expression are removed—large classes, rigid curricula, and overbearing authority in particular, the way is made clear for students to openly voice their true perspectives. This is made much more likely if they are given the opportunity to meet one another and come to feel that they are among friends rather than strangers. One useful way of facilitating friendliness is to begin a class by getting people to mix and mingle and introduce themselves "as if they were at a party." I often ask new classmates to talk to at least five new people and to tell them something interesting about themselves that the others would not be able to tell by looking at them. It can be a useful way of unfreezing expectations of how a class will be from the outset. By removing the common classroom introductions of "Hi I'm Emma and I'm an accounting major," learners bring their real personhood into the classroom and enter it as themselves and not as a "student." This is essential as emergent learning has to involve the whole person in a genuinely personal engagement.

Feeling that one is in a safe and friendly environment allows tentative thinking to emerge and when a learning process is based upon expanding understanding beyond narrowing limitations, all movement outward is necessarily tentative. This is inevitably so given that any emergent expansion takes us beyond the boundaries of what is already known and into the terrain of the unknown where we can no longer be certain. Moving beyond our existing zones of comfort makes us feel not only uncomfortable but vulnerable, as our habitual patterns of defense no longer apply. To offer up the tentative *is* to make oneself vulnerable and it will only occur when there is an intimate level of trust and respect in the classroom. Having people discuss issues in small groups of four or so is immensely helpful in opening up conversation, particularly if the time allotted allows for some broader conversation. Shifting these groups as regularly as possible builds a more extensive sense of intimacy as participants meet each other and find common ground in new groups. Working in such safe settings quickly allows students to find their voice and shape perspective as it emerges in the group as a whole. Creating maximally friendly environments is then a basic precondition for collective understanding to emerge.

To work well, education in this mode requires that both the teacher and the learners be genuinely open to what others have to say and that they are capable of responding to all that might emerge in non-offensive and non-defensive ways. The realities of opening up the learning process are that as a teacher, one never knows exactly what will emerge in any given conversation. When openness reigns, a tremendous range of ideas, thoughts, feelings, and opinions come to the surface and there are constant curveballs—the "disruptions" of normal classes—that have to be dealt with. Openness can be challenging to work with but it is also singularly satisfying as managing its dynamism calls for a range of spontaneous skills rarely used in more mainstream teaching.

Challenging Questions

One of the fundamental principles of educating *for* responsibility is that it aims to take people beyond the limitations of what is presently known and into the realm of the unknown. In this space uncertainty and confusion lurk and the purpose of emergent learning is to bring certainty and clarity to bear in these more expansive realms. In making sense of the unknown, students will at first be guided as much by emotion and intuition as pure rationality and this adds a rich complexity to what emerges into open discussion. In order to structure what could easily otherwise veer towards chaos, learning is contained and directed by employing carefully targeted questions. These questions provide the structure of a course of learning and guide learners' attention through a series of sequential themes—until they arrive together at a more expansive and responsible point of view.

Educating *for* responsibility requires going beyond limitation in a number of realms and useful questions extend student thinking beyond the limits of shortsightedness, narrowmindedness, and superficiality in particular. These deficits lie at the epicenter of our current malaise and it is reasonable to say that the various systemic crises we now face (in climate, food security, energy, and so forth) all emanate from the deeper crisis of our collective small-mindedness To release the potential for exercising a more mature responsibility, each of the three dimensional deficits mentioned needs to be confronted. The themes and questions that guide learning *for* responsibility are designed to specifically stretch learners' thinking beyond these root restrictions. By being challenged to answer a series of core questions, more farsighted, broadminded, and deeply considered perspectives can be developed.

Useful questions work not only to expand understanding but also to holistically integrate it and specifically asking for feelings, thoughts, observations, and previous experience to be included makes the search for answers real and engaging. It also encourages the broader intelligences of emotion and direct seeing to add to understanding, so connecting more realistically with our natural ways of growing into responsibility. Deliberately bringing these forms of intelligence to bear makes the process of developing realistic perspective not only interesting, but also confirming and moving.

Yet all points of emerging conclusion are only ever tentative in an emergent learning model, and each provides the opportunity for further exploration. Most of the stream of subsidiary questions that I ask a class are in spontaneous response to poorly formed conclusions. These often highlight exactly where and why students are holding back or are stuck. Good questions that take students to the heart of their confusions to help resolve them are powerful learning tools for keeping teaching active and responsive. Questions can be given for personal reflection, for journal writing, for small group discussion or for formal assessment depending on the level of attention they merit. Thus, although the central structure of a course is set by a small number of core themes and questions, it is supplemented by a constant stream of new questions as each group follows its own path to the collective destination.

There are then a variety of uses to which good questions can be put. They can be used to challenge premature conclusions, to extend thinking on a variety of dimensions, to consolidate understanding, and to undo confusion. I will give many examples of how questions can be put to effective use in the pages that follow, but here it is important to note the broader implications of shifting teaching practice away from providing all the answers to asking the critical questions. This is in fact a fairly revolutionary shift and it is the defining dynamic of the present approach. When learners are asked to answer questions that extend beyond their habitual boundaries of consideration, a challenge is laid before them to become authoritative in their own answers. In traditional teaching, what is authoritative always lies elsewhere—in the teacher, in the literature, in expert opinion and is passed on for passive acceptance. In educating *for* responsibility the challenge is not to passively accept authority, but to actively develop it. The teacher's role therefore reverses to become not the authority, but the *tester of authority*—as students' conceptions are challenged and vigorously tested for adequacy.

Working with an appreciation that responsibility is a potential inherent in all learners, there is little need to force upon them the opinions of others as to what their responsibilities should consist of. Young people are, after all, particularly resistant to being preached at in such matters. The questions that create the core of an education *for* responsibility require that young people come to their own conclusions and are deliberately written to deny them the opportunity to substitute expert opinion for their own considered response. If learners are asked to define the future world they really want to live in, one that will be by their own definition better, they can quickly develop for themselves a rigorous vision of what their responsibilities to the future are. If their answers are tested, critiqued, and amended in response to new questions as they emerge, they move towards becoming resilient frameworks against which personal and collective action can be meaningfully measured. The core questions in the first phase of learning aim to bring these evaluative frameworks to the surface so that they can be tested and used. Given that content is self-generated, these frameworks have a power and resonance that is deeply meaningful and resilient.

In this context, I also ask what people think the essential qualities for creating this better world are. In other words, what values must we enact, what virtues, or progressive characteristics have to become our shared "code of conduct" if we are to help bring this better world into being? As answers emerge and find form, a critical framework develops within which broad rules for responsible conduct are discerned. If a group says it wants to live in a more sustainable and inclusive world (as they generally do) then they might reasonably also conclude that it will take greater respect, compassion and self-restraint to get there. These self-generated conclusions end up being as rigorously worked out as any formal philosophy and they resonate with those who actively developed them in ways that no externally forced perspective ever could.

In the second phase of learning, additional core questions are asked that place the learner within the frames of reference they have already developed in order that current levels of personal responsibility can be assessed. We then move to looking at what happens when we extend our responsibilities in action so that we practice both thinking and acting more responsibly. Learners are asked to what extent their current lifestyles facilitate or debilitate the better world they believe we should work towards. We ask why our actions are not more harmonious and what really is holding us back from more responsible conduct. We look at how well we rate when we evaluate ourselves against the responsible potentials for compassion, respect, care, and self-restraint. We ask what we do in our lives that exemplify these virtues and how we could enact them more extensively. Questions like these challenge all learners to reflect deeply upon their current choices and place their actions in a more broadly considered perspective. This is the basis for consolidating a resilient and empowering sense of responsibility and it can be a genuinely transformative experience as students are asked to transcend the limitation of partial views and come to see their responsibilities in a wholly new light.

Constant Discussion

The dynamics of expansive spaces and challenging questions create an exceptional energy and the engagement with learning that results is usually highly enthusiastic. As learners warm to expressing themselves and applying themselves to answering really meaningful questions, a torrent of tentative and partial perspectives enters the room. There is no way this range and diversity can be fully debated if students are limited to talking only through the teacher. But such complexity *can* be dealt with if the process is decentralized and learners freed to debate, argue, and resolve issues by talking with each other. Discussion is then, a third critical condition in educating *for* responsibility as it unleashes the powerful potential of collaborative learning and collective advance.

The standard model of talking *at* and not *with* learners forgoes a vast and varied perspective when it denies students voice. In some of the classes I teach, there will be people from over 20 different countries. There will be people from several religious traditions and many agnostics. We will have gay and straight students, optimists and pessimists. There will be mothers, people who have lost close friends or relatives and at least a few suffering from a variety of conditions—both mental and physical. The depth of wisdom and the breadth of experience present is often far greater than we appreciate when we deal impersonally with students. If this variety is instead capitalized on and encouraged, rapid advances in learning can be achieved.

A richness of perspective can, however, be difficult to manage and balance is brought to bear by using group discussions to find focus as we work towards essential collective agreements. To illustrate, if for instance a teacher were to ask a group of 50 learners to identify the critical defining characteristics of a better world, they would be swamped by an unmanageable torrent of vigorously competing ideas. To keep this diversity but make it workable, it is useful to ask students to resolve initial differences and find consensus in shared summative answers. The criterion of consensus is immensely powerful in this regard and it very efficiently and effectively consolidates diversity into more essential and fundamental viewpoints. When asked to find consensus, learners are placed in a dynamic and highly energized process. If the questions asked are meaningful, such as to define the qualities of the world you want to live in, and if learners are given proper time to think about it, they enter group discussions with well-thought through positions. The power of finding agreement with others is that it brings into play a whole host of wider abilities—all of which are key to building an expanding responsibility. In order to find agreement learners have to articulate, negotiate, listen, defend, learn, respect, adapt, compromise, and cooperate. Each of these is a valuable skill in its own right and as a group works to refine its thinking, learners are forced to dig deeper into their assumptions as habitual thinking is challenged and more defensible perspectives demanded by their peers. This is the essential work of any truly educational experience and the beauty of activating group debate is that these useful dynamics emerge spontaneously to advance learning through the simplest of arrangements. A self-directing dynamism is released when we shift to working collaboratively as it opens up the natural energies that drive active learning. Young people want to explore what it means to be responsible and they want to openly discuss these issues with their peers.

In discussion, emergent learning receives its testing and a rapid deepening and broadening of perspective can be quickly achieved.

I ask students to discuss questions in small groups almost every time we meet as it keeps the atmosphere lively and allows learners to practice listening, negotiating, and working with others. Building in discussion time for small groups allows students to regularly speak their minds in intimate settings, but in general the whole philosophy underlying educating *for* responsibility sees all time together as potentially collaborative discussion time. As learners develop the ability and inclination to raise objection, difference, uncertainty, and doubt, spontaneous questions become a much larger part of the classroom dynamic. These questions help create new group conversations and serve in particular to frustrate the temptation to lecture students at length. Among other things, this conversational dynamic ensures that what is being taught remains maximally relevant and is genuinely meaningful and useful to learners. Through cultivating a constant dialogue teachers and learners stay connected, and work *with* each other to a degree rarely found under standard approaches.

****

These three elements of open spaces, expansive questions, and constant discussion provide the essential framework for an effective education *for* responsibility. In safe spaces students are liberated to voice and test their developing perspectives free of the fear of condemnation or belittlement. With creative questions emerging ideas, raw feelings, and partial perspectives can be pulled out, analyzed, and challenged in order to facilitate a more robust view of responsibility. And through constant discussion, disparate views can be forged into resilient shared conclusions with great efficiency. In reality these elements are inextricably involved with each other and they work synergistically to facilitate a constructive emergence of perspective. Feeling safe to voice difference makes for deeper discussions. Working in intimate groups builds feelings of relationship and camaraderie. Group discussions generate new questions that stimulate new group conversations and so on. Once the dynamics start unfolding they build their own momentum and into this the usual ingredients of assessment, resources, and teaching content can all be mixed. But as we will see, these are always used as aids to emergence and not substitutes for it.

In conclusion, working with responsibility as an emergent capacity requires balancing spontaneity with structure, and freedom with form. Safe spaces, clear questions, and open discussion remove limiting barriers to expansion and lead learning outwards towards a more broadly, deeply, and essentially responsible way of being in the world. The ability to orchestrate the best balance of freedom and form comes from a constant sensitivity to what is unfolding and a spontaneous clarity as to the specific barriers that have to be overcome if learners are to develop a truly mature perspective. Properly applied, the end result is a process of great energy, respect, and relevance and when managed sensitively, it is one that students regularly describe as being transformative and life changing.

To understand how this can be the case, we need to see how these foundational principles can be used to build a coherent course of learning. The next section offers a template for how these elements might be combined in an educational experience of around 36 contact hours. Remembering though that these techniques are eminently adaptable, they can be separated or curtailed to suit much shorter applications. For the particular circumstance of a university course in responsibility however, the following is tailor-made.

CHAPTER 2

Designing and Implementing a Full Course in Educating *for* Responsibility

Phase One—Defining Responsibility

- Core Theme # 1—Articulating Visions of a Better World
- Core Theme # 2—Identifying the Values Needed to Build a Better World

Phase Two—Practicing Responsibility

- Core Theme # 3—Evaluating Personal Responsibility
- Core Theme # 4—Expanding Personal Responsibility
- Core Theme # 5—Creating Responsible Businesses for a Better World

The function of education is to teach one to think intensively and to think critically. Intelligence plus character—that is the goal of education.

Martin Luther King

Much education today is monumentally ineffective. All too often we are giving them cut flowers when we should be teaching them how to grow their own plants.

John W. Gardener

The preceding section on how safe spaces, challenging questions, and frequent discussion work to draw out understanding runs the danger of being seen as a process occurring in isolation from academic study and research; but, that is not the case. In practice, emergent learning is supported by a constant stream of readings and other materials drawn from a wide range of sources. These are used to further extend thinking, aid integration, prompt imagination, and intellectually solidify learning. The pool of available materials is not, however, limited to the latest academic journals but instead, goes beyond this to include many engaging reports, books, documentaries, and Web sites—most of which are equally authoritative but more contemporary and broadly informative. A sample resource package is included in Appendix III for anyone interested. In beginning a course it is important to give particularly engaging materials to simulate thinking and draw students into a constructive interest.

When a class first meets, it is imperative to set a constructive tone by being as welcoming and friendly as possible. Learners need to be put rapidly at ease and explaining how the course will run, the expectations for involvement and the potential for learning are key. Respectful relationships begin with transparency and the operating principles and all expectations should be made clear but without being ponderous or authoritarian. Humor is a great icebreaker and if one can get a class laughing in the first meeting, then things tend to become much more relaxed and friendly. In unfreezing expectations about education as usual, having students introduce themselves and begin talking as whole people is very important in the formative stages of a course and the strategies mentioned above in the context of creating open spaces can be employed to good effect. All chances to get students talking and all opportunities to give encouraging support for what is contributed should be taken advantage of in the attempt to build a constructive and ongoing participation.

Learning time is devoted to two major phases of learning, each supported by extensive readings, some of which can be found in Appendix III. The first phase seeks to clarify what responsibilities a group sees as being important and the second seeks to put these self-defined responsibilities into more extensive practice. Each phase involves core questions and a series of exercises that vary in specifics from group to group.

Phase One—Defining Responsibility

Once the broad principles of a course have been briefly explained the process begins by asking learners the first of a series of questions designed to bring their values and ideals out into the open. The first question I often ask is: "Right now, do you think that the world is getting better or worse?" Learners are asked to take a few minutes to ponder this in silence in order that their thinking settles and focuses. After three or 4 minutes they are asked to write their conclusion down along with a few reasons that justify their assessment. It is an excellent opening question for a number of reasons. First of all, it is wholly unexpected and learners are usually taken a little aback by its directness and by its obvious importance. It is also useful in that it asks directly for the learners' *own* perspective and in doing this, it gives authority to their answers as only they can be experts on what they believe. But more importantly it invisibly activates ethical thinking as the criteria of "better" and "worse" are introduced and grappled with.

Students engage with this opening question enthusiastically and after developing their own thinking, they are invited to mingle with their peers and find a group of three others to join and debate with. The discussions are designed in part to have people meet each other and form friendships, so discussions can be fairly loose at this point. Group members are asked to ensure that each person speaks and that all are listened to attentively. The point is not to win an argument but to understand others' perspectives. With this explained, groups visibly begin to manage their own interactions in increasingly constructive and respectful ways.

After 15 or so minutes of usually highly vigorous debate, the class as a whole can be brought back together and a broader discussion can be initiated. This can be done in a variety of ways and it can be instructive to have the group divide physically into groups of "optimists" and "pessimists." The teacher can ask questions of individuals or these opposing groups as a whole, or allow some time for an open exchange but the most effective response will always depend on the energy in the room. The basic aim of this first thinking exercise is to loosen the class up for discussion and every perspective offered should be welcomed and constructively integrated into the emerging flow of ideas. This process works well for an hour-long class and as an introductory session, learners usually leave feeling intrigued and positive.

Core Theme # 1—Articulating Visions of a Better World

When discussing the critical role of good questions in bringing emergent perspectives into the open, mention was made of a series of core questions that direct attention and structure learning. These aim to stretch students' consideration outwards beyond narrow, short, and shallow limitation and toward essential anchoring points, helpful for exercising mature judgment. The opening exercise above works to prepare the ground for the first core question that students are asked which is what exactly does a better world look like and what qualities define it?

In the preceding exercise that begins the course, students show a ready willingness to judge improvement or decline but most of these judgments are very partial and only vaguely thought through. Many will judge on the basis of only a few observations or on the basis of a raw hunch but importantly, all have an opinion on the matter. The ultimate goal of the first core question which stretches thinking into the future is to refine thinking until the group can clearly discern where our genuine responsibilities to that future lie.

To continue the process I might conclude the first session by saying something like this:

> *Thank you all for your input on this question of whether things are getting better or worse in the world as we look to the future. You can see that there are a wide range of perspectives on the matter and what I will ask you to do now is to try and consolidate these various ideas into a more rigorous understanding and this begins with defining what exactly it is you mean when you say that the world is getting better or worse. In other words what criteria are you using to judge our progress or regress?*
>
> *Between now and our next meeting, I want you to spend some time bringing these implicit criteria to the surface and an effective way of doing this is to try and create for yourself a list of five or six definitive*

qualities that capture the essence of what a better and worse world will look like. Think of this in terms of list of single words or short phrases which taken together capture the heart of what you believe a better and worse world involve. These criteria should be as clear and comprehensive as you can make them and should be an honest and genuine expression of what you think makes for a better and worse future.

I will not make any suggestions for what types of criteria might be applicable as I know from experience that these will be repeated back to me. What I am challenging you all to do is to develop your own perspective and to bring this to class in order that it may be intelligently discussed and compared with the views of others. Thus, you need to take some time—and at least half an hour is needed—to quietly and deeply reflect on the type of world you want to see emerge over the next two decades and the type of world you want to avoid seeing emerge. Write out a list of five or six adjectives that capture the essence of these future states and which define why they are better or worse. Once you have done this, find two people whose opinion you respect and ask them if your list of criteria accord with their thinking. Where appropriate, you can change or amend your lists in response to these conversations.

The lists you finally develop should be brought to class as two sets of criteria—one defining a better world, one that you would like to see come into being, and the other defining a worse world—one that you do not wish to see eventuate. Next time we will break into groups to discuss these lists and begin to work to find a common agreement on where we should, and should not be heading as we look to the future.

****

In the next meeting students arrive with well-considered lists and are keen to find out what others have developed. The class is then asked to form into new groups of four (in order that they may share with new people) and they are given around 20 minutes to work toward finding consensus on the most definitive characteristics of a better and worse world. At the end of this time, groups are asked to finalize a working list and then each member takes this partial conclusion into a new group of four where it can be further harmonized with the collective opinions of others.

These discussions are always rigorous and energetic as students bring into play their deeper values and their real cares. The first 20-minute discussion rarely reaches conclusion and this is useful in taking a spirit of ongoing enquiry into new groups. During the second iteration though, things begin to become clearer as diverse opinions and overlapping themes are aligned, condensed, and agreed to. This double discussion works well in the 2-hour classes I have scheduled each week (I teach in a 3-hour format with one 2-hour meeting and one 1-hour meeting with learners) but this exercise can be spread over two 1-hour meetings quite readily.

At the end of the second class I ask each group to write down their concluded lists and I collect these in so they can be worked on before the next meeting. The discussions that students have had concerning the nature of better and worse worlds advance toward conclusion very effectively as diversity is condensed into essential shared perspectives so the lists that groups hand in overlap to a considerable degree. The primary work for the teacher at this point is to help find clarity among the varied themes. Thus, the raw lists are collected and a working interpretative summary made. The end sought is ideally a set of concise criteria that can form continua of opposing states. Better and worse are generally thought of in opposing terms and as a result, the central criteria that the groups articulate often fall into basically bipolar forms as a better world is defined as say, sustainable and a worse one as unsustainable, or a better world as more peaceful and a worse one as more filled with conflict. The working summary created by the teacher is then taken back to students as a possible representation of what they are collectively saying and learners argue for or against it until it settles into a final and collectively endorsed vision.

An example of how this looks in practice is probably useful at this point to give a flavor of the themes that arise and the challenge of integration. One recent class, after engaging in two group discussions, presented me with this list of criteria for defining a worse world (pulled into thematic groupings to be fed back to the group).

Characteristics of a Worse World (Will have more...)

Climate change/Climate instability
Environmental problems

Increased use of natural resources

Unsustainability

Global warming

Non-renewable resources running out

Resource depletion

Desertification

Irreversible damage to life on earth

Depleted oceans

Reduced biodiversity

Corruption/Increased corruption

Political corruption

Corruption in business

Increased inequality

Unfair distribution of wealth

Famine/Poverty

Increased inequality of power

More disparity

Severe unemployment

Social division

Conflict

Violence and warfare

Competition for resources

National insecurity

Increased tension between government and people

Greater crime

More murders and wars

Terrorism on a global scale

Rise in extremism

Decreasing freedom

More police presence

More surveillance

Disempowerment

Forced conformity

The suggestive categories here are that a worse world will be increasingly unsustainable, corrupt, divided, violent, and unfree. Posting the list and then asking if this is indeed what the group is saying allows for the next stage of learning. At this point though, it is instructive to cast one's eye back over the above list and appreciate the range of important topics that have already been discussed within the class. It is an admirably diverse list of themes to have been considering.

Reaching a final rigorous conclusion as to the future we want and do not want can take a considerable time if students introduce new ideas out of the blue, or insist that pet concerns be retained in a larger agreement. However, all such input adds to and tests perspective and eventually a final listing is agreed to. The power of this agreement is that it is reached actively and therefore has much resonance and depth. The emerging content is not only understood but *owned* and this gives it an authority that is uniquely powerful.

In the case of the criteria outlined previously (for a worse world), these were eventually combined with their positive equivalents and worked to a final set of dimensions, which were:

Better world	Worse world
Sustainable	Unsustainable
Inclusive/Equal	Divided/Unequal
Peaceful/Secure	Violent/Insecure
Free	Constrained
Having integrity	Corrupt

Once students affirm that the criteria they have worked to articulate really do capture their thinking, the role of the teacher shifts to challenge and test the legitimacy and depth of the emergent conclusions. So, when groups agree that sustainability is a key criterion for a better world, asking whether they mean by this a simple ticking over of nature, or a regeneration, or a deep thriving, brings increasing clarity and depth to thinking. If equality is raised as a key principle, just what learners meant by this can be explored by asking how this differs from equity, or how willing they would actually be to live with the reduced flow of resources that true equality would require. If peace is held up, or tolerance, these can be queried and questioned as adequate means to counter abuses of power, for example, and difficult to assimilate counter-examples can be posed to firm up and extend thinking. The specifics will of course depend entirely upon the ideals raised and the flow of discussion at any particular point in time. However it is essential to rigorously test and challenge all emerging conclusions as this forces the group to dig more deeply to defend their conclusions in vigorous debate. This is a hugely important skill for developing a resilient capacity for responsible action.

Throughout this process emergent ideas are constantly pushed to form deeper, broader, and more extensive perspectives and by its conclusion, learners have begun to develop rigorous moral defenses for responsibilities that they truly care about. In defining a better world for themselves, learners develop a clear set of ideals which, because they are cared about, contain an implicit responsibility to work for their thriving. Having accomplished this, along with a host of other learnings, we leave the discussion of our responsibilities to the future aside and engage a second core theme relating to our responsibilities in the here and now.

Core Theme # 2—Identifying the Values Needed to Build a Better World

If learners can actively articulate a meaningful set of ends as they do above, then attention can shift to considering the related question of what individual qualities need to be cultivated and spread if we are to attain these ideal future outcomes. Thus, if we want a world that is more sustainable, equal, tolerant, and peaceful, how do we need to act? What qualities or virtues need to be uppermost in society if such harmony is to reign? This line of questioning aims to clarify the means to the ends that have been identified in the preceding discussion and the means of achieving a rigorous answer runs in parallel to what has already been done.

In introducing this question I generally explain the logical connection between ends and means and then ask the group to take a few minutes to silently reflect on their own. I then ask them to form new groups and try to find common ground on what the most essential personal qualities are for building a collectively better world. These are again formed into simple lists of core qualities that can be shared, negotiated, and aligned. Instructions to the class are along these lines:

For the past couple of weeks we have been working to develop a vision of the type of world you all want to live in. This is one that is essentially more sustainable, more just, more inclusive, more tolerant, and more peaceful. These are fine and generally acceptable ideals and they do represent what most people aspire to. But if we are to bring such a world into being it will require the exercise of our best personal qualities and potentials. In other words improving the world around us begins with improving ourselves and the ways we think and act. What I want us to do now is to see if we can pinpoint the key qualities, the most important values or the critical virtues that we need to cultivate and spread in order to build a better world. What must we become like if we are to succeed?

As with trying to define the qualities of a better or worse world, I will avoid giving any particular suggestions as these will again be given directly back to me. I want to know what you think these essential personal qualities are and again if you can be as honest and open as possible this will make our conclusions genuine and meaningful. What I would like you to do is the following.

I want you to take a few minutes to think for yourself about what you believe these critical personal capacities are. After a few minutes write down a short list of five or so qualities and then form a new group of people you have not talked with before and share your thoughts. Make sure that everyone presents their ideas and that you listen to what is being said and then work to develop a consensual list. As in previous discussions you will find that there is much overlap and much difference too in what you all think and you should work to find the core of what you collectively see as being of critical importance.

****

I would again give around 20 minutes for these discussions and at the end, ask the groups to write down a working list that represents their thinking at this early stage. These would be collected in order that they can be worked on before the next meeting. (In the structure that I work with I would do the above exercise in a 1-hour meeting and the follow-up in a 2-hour one.)

Before the next meeting the group lists are gathered and made into several sets of cards each containing a single quality raised by the groups. With 10 groups of 4, this will produce around 50 individual cards in each pack (10 lists of 5 criteria). These sets are then taken to the class to be sorted into meaningful categories in larger groups through which essential agreement on a final list of critical qualities can be reached. I will usually break the class into larger groups of eight for any exercise like this as it changes dynamics and calls for greater collaboration. As a kinetically involving exercise, it is amenable to larger numbers of participants and enlivens proceedings.

The pack of cards that each group gets might look like this example, which is taken from a recent iteration of this exercise (each criterion has the number of times it was mentioned by different groups beside it and there would be this number of cards relating to it in each pack).

Characteristics to Bring About a Better World

Compassion/Empathy—14 mentions/cards
Generosity—10 mentions/cards
Open-mindedness—8 mentions/cards
Honesty—7 mentions/cards
Selflessness—4 mentions/cards
Kindness—5 mentions/cards
Forgiveness—3 mentions/cards

(And one or two mentions/cards for each of the following—accepting, positive, proactive, tolerant, optimistic, humble, self-disciplined, wise, free-thinking, active, considerate, motivated, and frugal.)

Again, the thing to appreciate here is that all of these topics have already been involved in deep discussion as learners grapple with defining them and seeing their relationship to other qualities and potentials. The discussions even to this point have been impressively broad-minded in their scope. In structuring the next stage I would introduce the categorizing exercise as follows.

I want you now to break into larger groups of eight or so people in order to resolve the complexity and difference of opinion groups wrestled with in our last meeting. I have here 6 identical packs of cards and on each card there is a single characteristic that a group raised as being of critical importance for building a better world. Together these cards contain all of the qualities that all groups mentioned so they are a comprehensive set of criteria. What I want you to do now is find a space where you can lay these cards on the floor and sort them into summative piles. That means that whatever terms you find repeated or which you believe cover the same theme should be placed together as a single concept. Those that are different should be separated. The aim is to end up with a small set of 5 or 6 qualities that your group believes captures the most essentially progressive qualities necessary for building a better world.

It is important before you begin though to note that the larger groups that you are now forming can often exclude some from the discussion as a few come to dominate the proceedings. Please make sure that your group keeps this in check and allows everyone's voice to be heard and considered.

****

This way of engaging students with the same essential task of finding consensus is valuable in that it brings novelty and movement into the room. As students stand around, change position, bend down to rearrange, and stand back, a vibrancy comes into play that is most enjoyable for all concerned. And because learners are working once again to clarify their own emerging ideas, they are highly engaged and energized in discussion.

After about 20 minutes I stop the deliberations and ask that all groups create one pile of qualities that are *essentially* positive and another that are not so but whose value depends on how they are used. In other words I ask them to separate out essentially virtuous qualities from instrumental ones, such as determination, resilience, creativity, intelligence, and innovativeness for the simple reason that each of these is of as much use to the tyrant as they are to the saint. It is useful to do this midway through the deliberations as learners commonly get bogged down with how these qualities fit at about this point in the proceedings. By allowing them to be confused for a while, the clarity of the resolution is made much more memorable and meaningful. Once the pile of contingent qualities has been put to one side, the shorter lists quickly come together with a little more time.

At the end of the meeting, discussions will be brought to a close and the conclusions of each group collected to be collated and brought back to class as a working summary of student perspective.

In this example, the group eventually settled on the following dimensions as being the essential ones when it comes to acting responsibly to create a better world:

Constructive values	Destructive values
Compassion	Carelessness
Generosity	Greed
Respect	Disrespect
Honesty	Dishonesty
Self-restraint	Self-indulgence

Once this is agreed to in open discussion of the same form engaged for the first core question, the accepted group conclusion is vigorously tested by the teacher to iron out its weaknesses and deepen its veracity. Thus, if a group claims that developing more honesty is critical to building a better world, asking about the limits of this or what exactly is meant by it is critical. If respect is seen as being key, then respect for whom—for racists, for murderers, for those who exploit others? Or if it is generosity, how does this fit with the tendency to freeload or take advantage of others' generous natures?

At the end of such vigorous challenging, learners will develop for themselves a deeply considered code for responsible conduct—one that has genuine applicability. Because it articulates their own perspective, it is owned and maximally meaningful and highly resilient too after its rigorous trial by fire in groups of varying sizes. The final list of progressive means complements the groups' ideal ends and comes to form a rigorous set of criteria that further clarifies what it means to be responsible in a larger and more carefully considered perspective. In a typical conclusion, students will reasonably argue that preparing for a responsible future requires a more skillful enactment of our inherent potentials for respect, restraint, compassion, generosity, and wisdom. That these are important and why is understood at a deep level and these qualities can be used from this point on as a measure of how responsible action is—across a whole range of domains. The conclusions clearly accord with most ethical schools of thought but none have had to be forced upon learners. Given the opportunity, learners can bring these out from within themselves and this is deeply satisfying.

Taken together with the articulation of responsible ends, the criteria that define responsible action allow young people to meaningfully mea-sure the responsibilities of businesses, the impacts of products or policies, the direction of media or any other phenomenon by the extent to which they facilitate the identified ends of a more sustainable, inclusive, and safe world and the extent to which they employ the virtues of respect, com-passion, and honesty in action. The framework is compelling given it has been self-generated and it empowers genuinely critical thinking given that it identifies the most essential criteria a group sees as being of value. As we will see, this evaluative framework becomes particularly powerful when it is applied to learners' own lifestyles where many suddenly see that their own actions regularly deny both the ends and the means they have come to appreciate more astutely.

****

Throughout these early explorations, students work to stretch an inte-grated sense of responsibility beyond narrow and short-term limits and this is facilitated by the fundamental dynamics of open exchange, rigorous questioning, and constant discussion. The simple outline above explains only the bare bones of what is actually happening in the classroom though, as learning is supplemented and consolidated by mini lectures, readings, documentaries, and subsidiary exercises. In the larger flow we will be debating fundamental ethical viewpoints, and referring to current affairs, politics, sociology, history, and psychology and structuring some simple exercises to encourage realism and practice responsible thinking. I will often, for example, ask students to write letters to themselves from the future describing what a day is like if things get better or worse. Or I will ask them to create a front page of the news 10 years from now reporting on this weeks' developments in a better or worse world. Exercises like these make the future more tangible and compelling and allow imagination some useful release.

Another common set of exercises I employ in this early stage of teaching involves putting the frameworks that students have developed to define responsibility to use by, for example, asking groups or individuals to identify five goods or services that build a better world according to the criteria raised by the group. Or to identify five businesses that are particularly destructive or constructive to the dream of building a better world. Such simple and short explorations give students the chance to practice responsible thinking in critical and creative ways and as with most skills, the more practice they are permitted, the more adeptly they can begin to perform.

Phase Two—Practicing Responsibility

The two-step process outlined here allows learners and teachers to quickly develop critical frameworks that can define key responsibilities and frame subsequent analyses. The conclusions are robust but they are still at this point largely *about* responsibility in the abstract. The most powerful dynamics of learning *for* responsibility come into play as these frameworks are applied to personal action and through this, our own enacted responsibility revealed. Turning attention explicitly toward the self gives the opportunity to actively work toward a more harmonious alignment and to experientially explore the challenges and rewards of enacting a more expansive potential. As this occurs the real dynamics of personal responsibility come to the surface often in fairly raw form as we uncover the compromises, the constrained reasoning, the defenses and the failings that always accompany curtailed responsibility. These dynamics are powerful but require careful management and again, good focusing

questions are of the greatest utility in bringing these barriers to the surface
and freeing the way for enacting an expanding responsibility.

As students begin to place their own conduct within the critical framework they have collectively developed, a good deal of energy is released as
things suddenly become far more pertinent and personal. There can be an
immediate tendency toward defensiveness and where this arises it is
important that it be made conscious and explored. The greatest traction
though can be gained when it is explained that the core questions now to
be addressed are not designed to create guilt or feelings of failure (although
these may legitimately arise) but rather to identify the common barriers
and potentials that we collectively share. If we can identify why and where
our own behavior fails to be adequately responsible, we will gain great
insight into why society as a whole remains as limited as it appears to be
when judged against responsible standards. A good deal of defensiveness
can be dissolved when this intention is made apparent and by directing
attention to a couple of core questions, students can begin to clearly see
the basic barriers to responsible action as they operate in their own lives.
Eventually also they can begin to glimpse the potential rewards that can
accrue from engaging with the world around us in more responsible ways.

The first set of questions focus on learners behavior in the here and
now thus undoing the common practice of only analyzing other peoples'
behavior in removed case studies. Learners are asked to look at their own
lifestyles from the perspective of the criteria they claim to care about. To
what extent does their consumption work against a sustainable world?
How often do they buy things that harm others and exacerbate
inequality? What are they currently doing in the way of giving money,
time, or effort to help others thrive? Or in the realm of progressive virtue,
what do they do on a regular basis that exemplifies compassion? How
honest are they and why are they not more so? And what happens when
they try to be more intentionally generous to others? The specific wording
of questions must, as always, be tailored to the specifics of the situation
but it is important to work toward two sets of related perspectives—
understanding the dynamics of personal and collective compromise and
understanding what happens when we work to transcend these limitations. The third and fourth core questions are designed to focus on these
dimensions respectively.

Core Theme # 3—Evaluating Personal Responsibility

I am surprised in most classes that so few anticipate that the frameworks they develop at the start of the course will be used to evaluate them by the middle of it. Some see it coming but for most it comes as a surprise and there is always a good deal of nervous laughter when it becomes apparent that they will have to be included in the analysis. Most know immediately that they will not fare well when put under scrutiny and are anxious about the implications for self-esteem. This is a healthy response but it is important to emphasize to students that discerning larger truths depends utterly on honesty and so any self-evaluation must be done openly and without fact-bending defensiveness. To aid this, specific revelations are more protected in order that students still feel free to express their common failings without condemnation from others. The shared perspective is built not then upon the specifics of individual failings, but on the shared conclusions learners reach as to why we all tend to compromise our responsible potentials in daily life.

To start this process, I might begin with something like this.

We have to this point been working to develop rigorous frameworks by which we can evaluate responsible action and in your own thinking this involves acting to facilitate a more sustainable, inclusive, respectful and equal world. Whatever actions lead toward this can be seen as being responsible and whatever actions lead away from it can be seen as irresponsible. You have also told me that you believe that acting respectfully, compassionately, generously, and honestly are also highly responsible, in large part because they are prerequisites for building an improving world. These criteria are good ones but fairly abstract. To make them real we need now to apply them to our own conduct and assess our own responsibilities against these sensible criteria.

I know that for some of you this comes as a worrying development but really, if we propose these as codes for others to follow we must accept that they apply as much to our own actions as they do to anyone else's. If we believe then that more sustainable, just, compassionate, and generous behavior should be forthcoming, we surely must believe that it should be forthcoming in our own lives as well. To not accept this is to head down a very shaky path indeed. What I want us to do now then is to put ourselves in the frame and take a good hard look at our own lifestyle and how it measures up in terms of enacted responsibility. Our consumption is a good place to start.

I want you to take some time to see if you can identify two things you buy on a weekly basis that most undermine the outcomes a better world involves. If we take the criteria of sustainability and equality, which were the two strongest imperatives raised, identify one regular purchase that you make which powerfully works against this desirable outcome. Explain as fully as you can why you buy this item, how you excuse it to yourself and how you feel about the inconsistency between your actions and your newly identified ideals. Similarly, identify one regular purchase that you think most egregiously works against the creation of more equality in the world and explain why you indulge, how you excuse it, and how the inconsistency between action and ideal makes you feel.

In doing this it is important to point out that the aim is not to beat yourself up or feel bad but rather to identify a range of contradictory actions and the patterns of thinking that keep compromise alive and well. It is important then to be entirely honest in answering these questions and we will bring the collective conclusions back to class to make sense of them. What this will allow us to do is identify the common barriers that hold us all back from engaging more responsible action.

****

There are a number of useful variations of this basic process of bringing attention to bear on personal responsibility. One is to have students complete an Ecological Footprint analysis and read the accompanying Living Planet Report to more accurately place their larger lifestyle in context. This is easy to do on-line and can bring to light the basic lifestyle habits that are most harmful in each student's case. It might be meat-eating or transport and the approach allows for the simple figure of "how many planets would we need if everyone in the world lived like you" to be revealed which is often compellingly vivid.

I generally find it more useful though to at least supplement this with a personal scrutinizing of one's choices to reveal personal limitation. If

petrol use and coffee use are barred as two obvious and somewhat hack-
neyed choices then learners have to think hard about how they consume
and the consequences of a whole range of their purchases in order to pinpoint their worst compromises. I ask that answers to questions be written
in the first person and that all non-defensively account for the discrepan-
cies they experience in their own lives. A detailed assignment sheet will be
provided (some examples can be found in Appendix I) and a short dead-
line will be set so that the momentum of learning is maintained. The
written answers students generate are all assessed in order to deepen
engagement and the dominant themes are quickly summarized and
brought back to the class for discussion.

Working in this way, common modes of excuse-making are revealed
as being almost universally present. In noting that their purchases of bottled water, industrial chicken, packaged snacks, and palm oil debilitate
efforts to bring a better world into being people commonly account for
this by denying knowledge, pleading habit, declaring an inability to relate
to victims or claiming that change will make no difference. These are the
excuses we all use to avoid more responsible conduct and bringing them
into awareness makes it possible to consciously challenge them and
become less prone to their conveniences. Once again the specific content
is generated by the learners themselves who bring their own active excuse-
making processes to the table. From the range of responses a critical essential understanding of how these dynamics work in our own daily lives
becomes vividly possible.

An example of these commonalities can be drawn from a recent
application where students' self-reflections revealed the following rationalizations in regular use (again with the number of discrete mentions
in brackets).

Excuses Used to Forgive Irresponsibility

Don't see the problem/Ignorance—10
Don't care/Am apathetic—13
Selfishness—24
Habit—23
Want to fit in/Fear of embarrassment—16

Futility—25
Can't see consequences—24
Don't know what to do—8
Will be more responsible later—6

Such a list again shows the breadth and depth of the discussions unfolding at the group level and produces a rich range of themes for exploration.

****

The example below comes from having learners evaluate the responsibility of their own behavior in relation to the outcomes they wish to see in the future. But it is equally useful to have them evaluate the extent to which their daily conduct accords with the list of responsible modes that they have generated under the name of progressive virtues. As an alternative to going down the path of comparing purchasing behavior to collective outcomes of value, I might ask a class to do the following.

What I would like you to do now, as we move to placing our own conduct within the framework of responsible action we have developed, is to actively and openly evaluate ourselves in terms of our own respectfulness, our own generosity, compassion, honesty and self-restraint. To do this I would like you to create a series of continua that are anchored by the positive virtues mentioned above at one end (the right hand side) and their opposite (however you wish to term these) on the left hand side. These scales should be 10 cm long and when constructed I want you to place a mark on each scale to indicate how developed you currently are when gauged in terms of respectfulness, generosity etc. The reason why I want them on 10 cm scales is that I can then calculate numerical averages that might be revealing.

To keep this real I want you to do two additional things. First of all, follow each scale with a brief explanation of why you think you deserve this rating. Do this by identifying for each virtue an example of your own behavior over the past two weeks. This time frame is important in order that we get a more accurate picture of how we do behave rather than how we have exceeded ourselves in the past. Great detail is not required for this but only a brief explanation of why the reported action is relevant to your self-evaluation. And because this exercise is not intended to have you beat yourself up over any perceived failings, I would like you to only raise incidents that involve you acting positively. I am not then interested in when you were greedy but rather when you were generous.

Finally, and also in the name of keeping things real, I want you to pick two people who know you well and get them to anonymously evaluate you on these same scales. You are not to read their evaluations as these are strictly between them and me. Please provide each person with an envelope and ask them to seal it before returning it to you. These others are not to make any comments but only to place a point on the continuum where they think you accurately are. The point of this is not to compare any individual evaluations but to aggregate the averages and see what this reveals.

****

Again a short time would be given to complete this and written answers worked with to bring out shared understandings and themes. It is again an approach that can be modified as the situation or group demands. One useful alternative is to take a subset of essential qualities and have students deal with these in more depth. I have, for example, taken generosity in a class that was particularly keen on this as a criterion for improvement and asked them to detail how much money they give to charitable causes in the course of a year. The discrepancy between what is intellectually recommended and what is personally followed is usually quite stark and students can be asked to reflect on and account for why they do not extend themselves more and what specifically is holding them back from giving. There are always compelling causes arising in the media and an exercise like this can be made more poignant if students are asked to investigate what help is being given by good institutions and how much is needed.

I have also taken compassion and asked students to watch footage of factory farming methods and ask the meat eaters (almost all) to account for their involvement in such a clearly non-compassionate industry.

Or one can focus on honesty and challenge students to be perfectly honest for a day. The permutations are potentially endless but the heart of this core question is to bring focus to bear on the unconscious inconsistencies of personal action and to bring to light the forms of reasoning we employ to forgive our less-than-fully-responsible choices. As the emerging conclusions are drawn from students' own thinking, they again have a valence and relevance that is compelling and conclusions can be tested, challenged, and validated by other readings and observations in sensitive but robust ways. In all of this, the key dynamics of open engagement, challenging questions, and constant discussion make a constructive progress both efficient and effective.

Core Theme # 4—Expanding Personal Responsibility

The fourth set of core questions follow logically from the one above and asks learners to experiment with changing behavior in order that it aligns more harmoniously with the responsible ideals they hold. This works particularly well if it builds directly on the observations of discrepancy that learners have already exposed in terms of their own roles as less-than-fully-responsible consumers and citizens. It is easy and useful then to ask learners to try eliminating the regularly destructive purchases they currently indulge from their habitual lives. If buying bottled water is clearly inconsistent with our responsibilities then we ought to desist. But saying this is one thing and doing it is entirely another. In asking people to not only *think* more responsibly but to *act* more responsibly a major but fully legitimate challenge is laid at their feet—one that brings their defenses into full swing and requires that their irresponsible siren calls be ignored and overcome.

By this point in a typical course learners are open to expanding their horizons to grapple with difficult questions. The preceding lines of enquiry have extended to connect with the future and with a variety of distant others. Now we extend consideration in a new direction, more deeply into the processes of the self in order to observe what happens when we try to actively improve our own conduct. The focus highlights deep-seated habits, weak excuses, selfish tendencies, and both unpleasant and pleasant feelings. In order to become more responsible in action, everyone has to learn to negotiate these powerful emotions and bring a more constructive harmony to bear. If learning can allow students to practice a greater responsibility and to experience the full consequences of this, a critical connection between personal thriving and collective thriving can be forged. This is the ultimate "glue" that binds us all to responsible action and makes it deeply rewarding. The aim in pushing people beyond their normal boundaries of consideration is to have them *realize* the weakness of the egos' excuses and the profound fulfillments than can come from aligning ourselves more harmoniously with the needs of the world around us. Here are two examples of how this challenge can be structured.

> *At this point we are beginning to see how difficult it is to live in harmony with the ideals we recognize as being worthy. We can see quite clearly where our individual and collective behaviors undo the world that we aspire to and we can recognize that our relative irresponsibility is kept in place by a variety of excuses such as not connecting action with consequence, not wanting to stray beyond our comfort zones and sheer convenience. This much is apparent, but what happens when we push these easy excuses aside and shift our behavior toward a more responsible footing? How does it feel? Is it painful or pleasurable? Is it empowering or disempowering? What thoughts arise to try and undo commitment and how can these be defeated? Is it possible to make a concerted and long-lasting change to our lifestyle in the name of responsibility? All of these are critically important questions and I would like to address them now.*
>
> *What I want you to do then is to take the items that you previously identified as being particularly problematic and stop buying them and using them in your life for a week. If you saw meat-eating as a major conflicting habit then challenge yourself to stop eating meat. If fizzy drinks in plastic bottles are your self-identified weakness, stop buying them for a week.*
>
> *Now this assignment is a particularly challenging one as it asks you to change your actual behavior. As you do this—and I want you all to really push yourselves to complete the task—all sorts of thoughts, feelings, and insights will come to the fore and I want you to make sense of these by writing on the following themes. What feelings do you*

experience as you deny yourself a habitual but harmful purchase? What thoughts arise to tempt you to compromise and how do you deal with them? What difficulties do you face and how do you honestly feel at the end of the week? Your writing should center on answering these questions as fully as possible in order that we can bring out the real dynamics of challenging our own responsibility. Finally I would like you to conclude by honestly evaluating the likelihood of your continuing to refuse purchases of this form and why you think this is so.

****

The question is formalized for writing purposes and specific guidance on how to execute it posted on line (see Appendix I). As with the previous set of questions that evaluate present status, the personal revelations central to each individual account are kept private as this boosts openness and the general conclusions across the group are brought out, questioned, and integrated into the larger architecture of the course. The results are always fascinating.

An alternative or an additional approach (because these work well in combination) is to practice going beyond current limitations by acting in more generous, compassionate, or respectful ways than one normally would. Thus for instance, learners might be asked to perform two genuinely generous actions over the coming week and to write in detail about how they feel before, during, and after the pro-social action. Or they might be asked to identify and then perform a series of compassionate actions in order that they push themselves beyond their normal boundaries—past their excuses and into a space where they can experience what it feels like to challenge and overcome limitation. When working with personal potentials, the question might be asked in this way.

(With a similar introduction as the previous one.) In the evaluations that you made of your own capacities you rated yourself as moderately accomplished on these virtues (6–8 out of 10) and generally gave convincing illustrations of why you rate as well as you do. The quality that you see yourselves as most accomplished in is that of generosity where you collectively scored yourself at around 7.5 out of 10 (this being gauged

by averaging self-placements across the group). But in this instance as with the other qualities you see as being important, you still see much room for improvement. What holds us back from acting in more constructive ways are a series of rationalizations that we employ to excuse our less-than-fully-responsible actions. What I want us to do now is to explore the real dynamics of challenging and overcoming these barriers and more fully expressing our potential for responsible action. What defenses arise as we try to move beyond our own comfort zones? How can these be challenged and what is it like to successfully find a greater harmony between the virtues we espouse and the actions we engage?

For this assignment I want you to push yourself to perform two genuinely generous acts over the coming week. These should take you beyond your usual repertoire of day-to-day behaviors and work to the significant benefit of another or of others. The range of possibilities is endless and part of the reason for asking you to act with a conscious generosity is that it changes the way we look at the world around us as we see it in terms of opportunities to be generous. Think very carefully about what you might do to push yourself—but not into terrain that would make you critically uncomfortable. In reality, the more you put into this challenge the more you will learn—and there is much to learn.

I would like you to please write 3–4 pages on what happened. You should include explicit reference to your thoughts and feelings before, during, and after the actions you choose and you should comment on what you believe the acts did for your relationships with the people involved. Focusing on your internal voices and emotions, write a clear account of what the experience of expanding responsible capacity has been like and how likely you would be to continue pushing yourself to be more generous in such ways.

****

This would be written up more formally and with more extensive guidelines as can be seen in Appendix I. Exercises of this form are fantastic things to engage as the learning they provoke becomes deeply personal and real. The outcomes vary depending on whether the focus is on collective outcomes such as sustainability or on personal potentials like generosity. However, it is desirable to involve both of these domains as this works to complement learning and the more practice students can get in acting with an expanded responsibility the better. In both cases, though a tremendous richness of insight is produced.

In bringing learners present weakness and potential strengths into such direct conflict, a deeply personal challenge is set. Most students find it extremely difficult to curtail their consumer choices and be intentionally generous for the sake of it. Almost all apply themselves wholeheartedly and the vast majority successfully completes the challenge. In the process they struggle with their egos and with their emotions as they battle habits, feelings of futility, and sheer frustration to accord with what they claim are their ideals. By asking for written reflections, a particular focus is brought to bear on these leading to considerable personal insight. Some discover that they are weaker than they thought they were, but many more realize that they possess strengths they never appreciated.

The most important learning that comes out of this focus however, is the discovery that in most cases exercising a greater responsibility is deeply satisfying and enormously potent in boosting self-esteem. When students struggle to resist meat-eating as their friends taunt them, and when they cannot find a conveniently unwrapped snack bar, or when they forget their refillable coffee mug, real emotions and frustrations emerge. The struggle to overcome limitation is a visceral one and it takes a lot of determination. Typically though, by the end of the week all of those completing the challenge feel genuinely proud of themselves. In the process of resisting poor habits they have also come face-to-face with many of the realities of the broader world that seem to conspire against responsible conduct. As, for example, simple mockery, or the frequency with which one stumbles across tempting ads for the very thing one is trying to avoid.

The positive benefits of acting responsibly are particularly evident when learners are asked to practice acts of generosity, compassion, or appreciation. As students recount making dinner for stressed neighbors, looking after children, volunteering time at a hostel, or helping a stranded motorist change a tire, they recognize the apprehension that precedes action and the temptations to turn around. They become aware of feelings of awkwardness and vulnerability as others' responses become hard to predict and they almost universally identify a tremendous good feeling as the result. The reception others give to displays of generosity are genuinely humbling and deeply moving for many learners. Their mothers cry when they give them a present or a thank you note for supporting them. Complete strangers shake their hands and tell them how good and kind they are. Common conclusions are that they felt like they were "walking on air," that they "held their heads high," that they were "proud of themselves" and generally deeply moved by their experiences.

The value of these self-generated conclusions is immense when it comes to opening up the potential for a consistent responsibility. We can argue all we like about how good it is in the abstract but it is not until people are placed in a situation where they can directly realize the benefits of acting maturely that its real benefits are appreciated. It is not always wine and roses though as some learners' efforts go awry, backfire, or go unappreciated. As with everything that emerges in the course of our explorations together as a group, these are equally instructive and questions relating to why suspicion arose, or why it is so important to be thanked for our generosity can be fruitfully explored and debated as they arise.

By the time students are working at this level of deep process, they have come a long way. They have defined for themselves a vision of a collectively better world, they have discerned the personal qualities necessary to get there, they have made a clear-headed assessment of their own conduct in light of these criteria and they have pushed themselves to improve. Along the way they have extended, deepened, and broadened their horizons and created a rigorous and integrative perspective on what responsibility entails and what it means to practice it. The final component of learning involves taking all of these expanding conclusions, insights, and realizations and extending them intentionally forward into the future in order that a central failing of modern business education be met head on—that of passing on potent skills without any guiding sense of how to responsibly apply them.

Core Theme # 5—Creating Responsible Businesses for a Better World

Most business schools devote the bulk of their energies to transferring technical skills of accounting, management, marketing, and so on and generally spend little time asking students to properly account for where, when, and how these can be responsibly used to build a better world. In the main, the responsibility of building a better world is left to the mysterious mechanisms of the market to resolve but such a faith leaves responsible intention undeveloped within the confines of a largely selfish conception of *homo economicus*. In working to assist our release of a fuller humanity, we need to create spaces in which future business people can explore how they might consciously align head, heart, and hands in maximally harmonious ways. The final core theme in educating *for* responsibility involves learners working together to develop realistic and genuinely progressive business ideas—ones which would be solvent, sensible, and highly conducive to bringing a better world into being.

This final core focus aims to stimulate student imagination as they contemplate their future direction. In many business schools, learners are given no time to imagine how they might put their skills to good use in the world and having the chance to find a satisfying alignment brings considerable energy into the classroom. This is once again in large part because it is such an obvious and meaningful question—that is how are you going to put responsibility into practice in the future as business people?

I generally ask people to work in groups to develop plans for real businesses that would directly facilitate a better world. The criteria set are rigorous and challenging and students are asked to show convincingly that their innovations will advance one or more of the ideal outcomes the class wishes to see eventuate. Groups are asked to demonstrate how the business is commercially viable and to address specifically how profit will be generated and used. The aim is to identify opportunities to act with integrity and to extend responsible intention into the future.

The challenge can be introduced in this way.

Now I think we have a much clearer understanding of what holds us back from more responsible action in the way of rationalizations and for most of us at least we have had a glimpse of how satisfying and meaningful it can be to act more considerately. It generally has positive outcomes for self-esteem, relationships and identity. Moving toward acting in ways more conducive to a better world is constructive and inherently gratifying. What I want to do now is to see if we can find alignment between the values we have been talking about and your own futures as business people. Is it possible to bring these values and this broadened sense of responsibility into alignment with real business practice? I think that your generation is fortunate in having to hand an ever-increasing array of new models as shifts in technology and culture open new opportunities for alternative ways of doing business. If you were to be part of a positive shift as a business person, what products, services, processes or other innovations could you develop that would be both practical commercially and progressive in actively bringing forth a better world?

I am going to ask you to work in groups of 6 or so for this and you can pick who you want to work with from the many people you have talked with over the weeks. I want you to develop clear and convincing arguments to support and validate your innovation and you must clearly show that it does considerably more good than it does harm. You should develop these ideas in collaboration and be able to present them to your peers as genuinely responsible business ideas. They will be assessed according to their creativity, their realism and the extent of positive impact that they will be likely to produce. You can write then with these criteria in mind.

****

When expanded in written form to give more structure, this challenge produces a tremendous amount of head-scratching and false starts as students struggle to think of how they might apply their business skills to create a more sustainable, equal, inclusive, and respectful world. How can a company operate to encourage generosity or compassion? These are difficult questions and groups typically go through cycles of frustration as ideas swell and are then punctured by thorny reality. Some groups quickly find good ideas but given that there is requirement to not copy an existing idea, most find it extremely difficult—and this alone is a valuable lesson in how much has to change to create a responsible economy. The common inability to make early headway although frustrating, is highly valuable in keeping students thinking, talking, and searching for answers and during this time I am careful not to give them too much guidance in the way of prospective answers. Rather, a good deal of time is spent both in class and outside it, meeting with students so that they can run their latest thinking past me as I question and test what is emerging—rigorously but sensitively enough to keep them heading in a constructive direction. When solutions are finally found, it brings a tangible satisfaction as skills and good intention come into a creative alignment.

How these are evaluated is covered in the section on assessment below but the sharing of often highly creative and meaningful business ideas ends a course in educating *for* responsibility on a positive and affirming note as learners are exposed to an imaginative range of good ideas that if put in practice, would begin a significant shift toward the kind of harmonious world they want to create for themselves.

****

Put together in sequence, the two phases of learning and the five core themes above create a meaningful framework within which responsible thought and action can be practiced. Learners work together to develop rigorous perspectives on what responsibility means, why it is important, how it can be practiced and why this is so challenging. The balance of freedom and form allows for targeted learning that involves the whole person and the open collaboration involved maximizes the intelligence available within any group of students. But the true benefits can only really be seen when one appreciates just how mature and complex the unfolding thinking that emerges is. This is evidenced in each meeting, and much of it in the writings that accompany each core theme and question. These writings are designed to prompt integrative and deeply reflective thinking and in them, learners display a diverse complexity of emerging perspective. In reflective writing the object is not to produce many similar approximations of a single model answer but rather to stimulate a wide variety of answers and insights. In balancing form and freedom of expression, a great diversity of ideas is generated and space created for learners to report on the *process of their learning*. This allows teachers to gain a far deeper understanding of how collective understanding is unfolding and the particular challenges that any individual learners are facing.

Open writing also allows for a more holistic pattern of learning as emotions, observations, and personal experience are brought to bear on the question. The end result is work that is not only a pleasure to read but also contains a wide diversity of expression and experience. Apart from the value of revealing common patterns of thinking, more open assessment also brings to light a large number of unique insights of tremendous value to advancing discussion. Considering a few samples of students' work will help illustrate the type of integrated learning that this approach facilitates.

CHAPTER 3

Learning Outcomes and Examples of Engagement

- Reflective Writing on Personal Inconsistency and Barriers to Improvement
- Reflective Writing on Challenging Inconsistency
- Reflective Writing on Practicing Kindness and Generosity

Education comes from within; you get it by struggle and effort and thought.

Napoleon Hill

The highest education is that which does not merely give us information but makes our life in harmony with all existence.

Rabindranath Tagore

Before proceeding, I should clarify that the core reflective writings students write on comprise a major element of assessment in most courses. Depending upon numbers and other commitments, I typically set 4 to 6 of these assignments which work in sequence to build a coherent multi-dimensional understanding of personal responsibility. These take a lot of time to read and feedback to classes but it is essential for the level of engagement that really makes the process work well. As can be seen in Appendix II, it is sometimes useful to create collective feedback documents as these allow commonalities to be fed back and save hours of individual comments. In most cases students like this format as it allows work to be returned quickly while the thinking it contains remains alive in the mind.

Given that the aim in educating *for* responsibility is to draw out a complexity of working perspective in order that this can be consciously improved, open assessments are useful. These allow students a wider and more integrated range of expression than is usual. As can be seen in the sample assignment outlines in Appendix I, it is useful to specifically call for feelings and observations to play a central role in whole-person learning of this kind. Writings of this form need to be well structured to avoid an unproductive dispersal of thought and to direct attention toward staying on the path of most fruitful enquiry. It requires a good deal of class time to explain the *purpose* of assignments and to deal with any confusion or concerns. In working collaboratively, the questions are usefully finalized with learners to ensure that the effort expended moves their learning forward as effectively as possible.

As can be seen by looking at the written versions in Appendix I, considerable structure is usually given particularly at the beginning of a course as many, if not most, students would not have been asked to write in this more open form before. Although some may be apprehensive, these feelings can be allayed and in my experience, almost all come to relish writing with an open and personal engagement. Many write far in excess of the suggested word limits for any given piece of work and this is fine if new revelations are coming to the surface and continuing to write is useful for the learner concerned. I see no reason for curtailing an unfolding realization simply to accord with an arbitrary word limit. Learners are encouraged to be as direct as they can be but where deeper themes open up and merit exploration, this should be allowed.

There are several things to note in the following samples of students' work apart from the ability to express views and integrate ideas. First and foremost is the constant sense of enquiry that characterizes them. Good, relevant questions grab students' attention and they work with a high degree of sincerity. Being drawn beyond the boundaries of what they normally consider, learners show an attentiveness to the world around them, which is refreshing and highly instructive. A measure of just how instructive it is comes in the regular mention of "*realizing*" important new things. This is the essence of successful emergent learning as the person comes to directly see relationships in, and with the world around them with far greater acuity. These realizations represent a resilient insight and are a form of concluding that leads to permanent learning and growth. To have a person change their consumption habits, or act more compassionately for a week places them in a novel situation where many new things can be learned and as it involves the whole person, these points of insight are often accompanied by real emotion. This natural and fully human dynamic is apparent in several of the sample writings that follow.

The emotional involvement of learning can lead some to express themselves in strong language, sometimes veering off into the use of an occasional expletive. This can be dealt with sensitively and in my experience it is a very rare occurrence. When shown respect, students reciprocate and generally restrain themselves from bad language but when they do stray, it is mostly an indication of strong feelings coming to the surface and I have little problem with it as such. In some ways it is also important to recognize that in their everyday discourse with each other young people will regularly speak in such terms and anything that aids the transition of ideas out to the broader realm of students' lives is useful. There is at least one example of this in the papers that follow. More importantly, there are many examples of learning extending outward to include others around them.

It is helpful to note also the extent to which learners seem to be on a path of exploration that continues previous perspective-building. This is a common theme when core questions logically flow from one another. The pattern of learning happens then not only within the present set of questions, but also in a much broader and spontaneously integrative mode. The most essential thing to note in these samples though is the diversity of material they produce for further investigation. If one imagines getting 50 assignments each as rich and unique as the ones below, then one can get a glimpse of how complex the overall learning can be.

The samples below were written in response to a range of questions that approximate the ones defined as core above but vary as to the particulars in each example. These are not selected on the basis of being of exceptional quality but rather, of broadly representative quality. One of the most gratifying aspects of educating *for* responsibility is that through exercises like these exceptional expressions of learning can become the norm.

Having said that though, I am tempted to begin with the exceptional as it demonstrates the outcomes sought in all reflective writing—that being the consolidation of a considered personal perspective conducive to an expansive responsibility. This was written in response to a compassionate exercise involving watching newsreel footage of an unfolding famine in the Horn of Africa and raising money to alleviate some of the terrible suffering caused.

Compassionate Living

Part One

They look so gaunt as in not human anymore. At least not the kind of human that I am used to looking at. Gaunt, oddly-shaped faces overpower their emaciated bodies as their dry skin hangs off each and every limb. Their eyes look huge—weirdly huge yet have no life dwelling in them. These poor children—poor in every sense of the word.

I'll be honest, I heard the news stories, I read the newspaper, listened to them speak on the radio about a massive famine in Africa and the intellectual part of my brain registered that 11 million starving men, women and children are holding onto life by a fraying thread. I know all of this. And yet, I am ashamed to admit, that is where my involvement with one of the world's worst famines ended. I did not immediately send money to World Vision or the like to alleviate the problem. I did not discuss it with my peers and colleagues. I did not even think too much about it. I did absolutely NOTHING. How could it be that I have so far ignored an enormous, important issue affecting the lives of millions of people? Is this how the Holocaust happened? Is this how 20 million Europeans let 5 million Jews die through murder, starvation and gassing?

When I was about nine years old I really got into reading—I loved books based on historical truth. "When Hitler stole Pink Rabbit" was a favorite of mine for about two years. Even as a child I felt sadness and confusion as to why people let these events occur. Why did no-one try their damned hardest to stop these massacres and injustices? And yet here I am, 12 years later, a by-stander and I can almost see my younger self confused and dismayed at my inability to act. Granted this disaster is not entirely man-made like the Holocaust but it is still a huge problem of epic proportions as millions of innocent people stand to lose their lives.

Of course, watching the YouTube videos of the famine in Africa makes you feel sad, sick, repulsed and frankly shocked. But all of these emotive responses are still not enough for a lot of people to be motivated to do something about it. Many of the papers we have read in class talk about the idea of being a by-stander. A non–whistle-blower, a go with the flow stationary idiot who dismisses ideas of moral thought and decisions for the greater good in favor of those rationalizations that serve self-interest. I want to buy 5 coffees a week and this costs me $20. Why would I give $20 to a charity that helps to alleviate the suffering of others when I could use it to buy my coffee each week? No-one else is doing that—they would think I was weird if I did. Besides, how much aid can $20 a week really buy? My impact is insignificant anyway…now where's my coffee? We are so quick to judge others and so quick to pass on the blame that we end up pissing our lives away focusing only on ourselves and a few others closely connected to us. We as humans are always ready to disown a problem, to pass it off as too big, too much, too out of our control. Our weird propensity to partake in blatant by-standing, coupled with most Westerners' unwillingness to engage in communal activities means we disconnect ourselves from each other. When you don't even care how your neighbors are doing living across from you, why the hell would you care about 11 million poverty-stricken Africans living thousands of miles away?

After my self-inflicted anger wears off and I read the remaining papers on "why we don't give more," I realize that my apparent inability to consistently think of other needy people in the world is not a characteristic unique to my personality. Apparently we are all inherently wired to not continuously think of others less fortunate than ourselves who are not in close proximity to us. We need a sappy story to capture our emotional sides. We need to attach one suffering child to a cause to get the attention of our thoughts. It seems so strange to me. Why can't we just be like that all of time? How much better the world would be if we had the instinctual ability to put the needs of others, or the greater good before ourselves.

Part Two

I will be honest, I hate asking for money. I have never even asked my parents for money unless I thought I really needed it. There is something I find so awkward about it—some underlying societal norm that dictates not to talk about and ask for money and it seems to hold me back from doing so. Hence I found the task of asking for donations quite difficult, even though it was for a legitimate and worthy cause. I still found ways to rationalize backing out of the money question. I thought that my mum would be a good place to start as she knows me really well and would know that I must have a very good reason to be asking for money. She was surprisingly quick in her response to say that she would be more than happy to donate to Oxfam. I didn't even have to blurt out my pre-made speech about the starving children of Africa who needed our help, and how collectively we can all make a small but meaningful difference.

I asked my sister too, to which she replied "I only have $40 left to last me until next payday. I can't afford it." I know that she has a terrible money sense and couldn't accumulate wealth to save herself. She laughed it off and said "I can't even look after myself, let alone an African child!" She was obviously trying to be funny but it made me realize that there must be so many other low to middle class families in New Zealand and throughout the developed world struggling to make ends meet in their daily lives. These households probably do not care or feel as though they are not able to give money when they are looking after their own families with the little money they do have.

The third person I asked was my best friend who is newly engaged. I felt bad asking her even though she has a full-time job and is a good saver, because I know that she needs to save around $20,000 for her wedding. Even so, she was more than willing to donate $5 to the cause. She had no idea about the starving children in the Horn of Africa and kept asking why it wasn't in the papers or on the news. She is not really one to keep up with the world news though. I was rather shocked that she did not know about this tragic event in the world. And it made me wonder how many other people out there are totally unaware of the situation. It is almost worse to be aware of the situation and yet ignore it as if it wasn't an issue. Ignorance is easy. Doing nothing is easy. It is actually doing something or feeling something about it that is the hardest part.

So I gathered my collected money and added to it from my own wallet. I was taken aback in class when it became apparent that we had raised over $2,000. I had been expecting around $200–300 to be raised and to get ten times that is amazing. I honestly felt very touched—because to see good come out of a group of people is to see humanity and compassion.

I have no doubt in my mind that this activity has definitely reduced my sense of futility. When I first started to watch those YouTube videos I felt a sense of worthlessness—that I could do nothing to help these peoples suffering. To know that we as a collective could actually alleviate the suffering of some of these people means a lot to me as a person. I now feel as though this positive outcome can be created by many communities and many collectives every day. It made me think that indeed we CAN make a difference. We can help, and yes I can help too. Excuses are easy to make when we feel we can rationalize our inability to help. Activities such as this one, collectively accumulating money to send as aid, smash straight through those rationalizations. Because our hearts and minds now understand what we have known all along—humanity has the unlimited ability to reach out compassionately to others, regardless of race, creed, religion or gender. Differences mean nothing as deep down we are all the same, humans with the capacity to love each other....

I think the greatest challenge in life is to be kind to everyone, the people you love, the people you hate, and the people who have no relevance to you at all. This is a huge challenge but I see it as the way forward to help alleviate world suffering after such crappy happenings. It is really important to know the limitations of your mind. Sometimes it's ok to be just a regular human being with bad days and good days. The challenge on these days is not to come up with new and innovative ways to change the world for the better, but just to be kind in your day-to-day dealings with the people you come in contact with. Kindness on a small scale can accumulate into kindness on a large scale. For me, it is about knowing how far I can take kindness each day. This past Tuesday was a day that kindness helped change the world for the better. Today might just be the day that kindness is a simple thank you, a genuine smile or a hug. Tomorrow may be another opportunity for kindness to spread to parts of the world that really need it.

I believe with every fiber of my being that kindness can and will change the world.

****

Now to the more genuinely representative. I have included in the following pages just a few examples of students writing in response to only a few questions in order to convey the results of working in these more expressive ways. Although it may seem that in many instances the issues grappled with are superficial and highly personal, the common processes they bring to the surface of students minds are profoundly important. Reflective writing brings a huge number of themes to the fore as learners grapple to understand what they have never considered. When collected across dozens of unique responses, the process provides a rich and textured flow of emerging realizations that can be explored as these few examples will hopefully show.

The writing that follows was in response to three basic questions, all from the second phase of learning for responsibility where the criteria for responsible action are applied to one's own conduct.

Reflective Writing on Personal Inconsistency and Barriers to Improvement

This is an example of reflective writing addressing the inconsistencies between personal consumption and stated ideals. Learners were asked to address aspects of current consumption and account for the excuses they make to forgive the lack of harmony.

Example i) Acting Inconsistently

Thinking of products that I purchase on a weekly basis was difficult for me. I am personally not much of a consumer. Outside of transport services and petrol I don't purchase much other than food and even this is purchased for me as I live at home. However, when considering my purchases and thinking about things I use on a daily basis that compromise my ability to say that I stand for a sustainable and inclusive world, two products stand out. They may sound clichéd, but in reality they probably have the greatest effect on my ability to stand for these values due my thoughtlessness in purchasing and consuming them. One of these products I am writing on right now (paper) and the other I have just had a drink of (coffee).

When thinking of sustainability and equality as values which we believe will build a better world we have to think about how we as individuals fit into the bigger picture and whether we, in our personal consuming, are bringing about positive change in the direction we desire. At the moment we have a world which is grossly divided; we have a Western world which has a standard of living which is massively disproportionate to the Third World where billions live on only a couple of dollars a day, or less. Our consumption not only causes this inequality, but it is also driving another form of inequality—unsustainability. We term it an unsustainable use of the globe's resources but it is in effect using the next generations' resources today. The outcome is today's generation having and the next not. As an individual living in a First World country that is devoted to the national religion of consumerism, I am part of making this inequality happen. And by doing this I am compromising my ability to stand for a more equal and sustainable world.

My consumption of paper is a good example of this. Every day I will print off something. I will use paper to make notes at university and eventually I will print off this assignment and hand it in. My friends have called me "a fanatic printer," never saying no to an opportunity to print a document of multiple drafts when making a document. While I am able to come up with many excuses for this consumption, the reality is that the use of paper has a direct effect on the sustainability of the planet. While paper is made primarily from trees which *can* be produced sustainably, a lot of paper is produced by the use of trees that are *not* being sustainably harvested, causing deforestation around the world. The paper that I use as a consumer may come from a sustainable resource, or it may not. However, it is commodity which is produced by the world market with my consumption directly impacting on the amount of paper products that have to be produced, whether sustainably or not.

Coffee is a product that also compromises my ability to stand for a more inclusive world as it increases inequality. Instant coffee is made from a number of products, with the beans actively producing inequality. While my consumption does help produce employment for people in developing countries, it does so in an inequitable way with me not paying the real value of what I am purchasing due to the cheap labor and poor working conditions involved in making the product. I have been helping exploit my fellow human beings. One of the values that I hold to closely is that of the inherent value of the human person. I believe strongly in the proposition that all people are created equal, but I see that our actions lead to what George Orwell wrote about in Animal Farm where "some are more equal than others." While I am not always sure where my coffee comes from, my thoughtlessness on the question is enough to show that I don't really care about the effects of consuming the product on other people in this world.

With my heart feeling the pain of my actions, my mind begins to come up with excuses which can clear it of any guilt.

The first excuse that comes into my mind is that I am only one person and what difference can one person really make? I understand that my consumption is creating damage but what is there I can really do about it? I am only one consumer out of millions doing the same thing. I really am insignificant in the overall scheme of things. Even if I were to reform my consumption habits, it wouldn't make a difference as everyone else will just continue what they are doing.

This excuse has a second part with my mind beginning to say that I am only one of many causing the damage, so am I really actually causing *that* much damage? I am totally insignificant in the overall scheme of things and in causing inequality and an unsustainable planet. In fact the laws of supply and demand basically say that in the short term supply is fixed. So if I were to stop consuming paper and coffee to the extent I am, all I would do is open the market up to someone else to continue the same behavior possibly at a cheaper price.

Another excuse that I then bring up is that of justifying the amount that I consume. "Surely there are others who are worse than me." When I look at my consumption levels I am probably below average when it comes to products such as coffee and probably close to average with print-ing paper. There are many others who are worse than me who should stop before I should have to. "Just think about all the big corporates and their consumption levels" I hear my mind say.

My mind then turns to another layer of excuses which are focused around the products themselves and my personal need for them. Socially, coffee is becoming more and more of a product which is needed by me to be able to fit in as a social being. It is in many ways replacing the position of the cup of tea in our society. Paper is used more and more, even though we have the technology available to minimize its use. Even here at the university we still require print-outs of assignments and we expect hand-outs in class of lecture notes. To stop using these products would mean that I would struggle to fit in and function as a member of our society.

Another excuse which takes a position in my mind is the economic effect of my consumption. If I were to stop consuming coffee, wouldn't that mean that the people who rely on my consumption for employment in Third World countries would become unemployed and a greater inequality would result as they lose their income source? If I were to stop consuming paper, what effect would that have on others in the global economy?

While there are elements of truth in these excuses (yes, I am only one person among millions; yes, if I reform my consumption habits it wouldn't make much of a difference; yes, these problems need solutions involving everyone) if we are going to make change, it has to start somewhere—with ourselves.

When I think of the realities of living unsustainably and the harm caused by inequality, my excuses look pathetic and my actions become inexcusable. If I believe that my consumption of paper and coffee are causing an unsustainable and polarized world then every cup of coffee and every piece of paper use is adding to it in one way or another. It doesn't ultimately matter how insignificant my usage is, the question must be put. Am I making the world worse or better?

Margaret Mead once said that a small group of people can change the world and that it is the only thing that ever has. This quote needs to be applied to ourselves. If we are going to change the world for the better, where sustainability and equality are core values of this better world, then we are going to have to embed these within ourselves and within our actions. The quote must then be applied to the communities we are involved in. To make the change to a more sustainable and just world we are going to have to work together, living out the ideals we believe in and working to make change across society. This will mean changing the economics of products so that they are produced sustainably and equitably—alongside changing the attitude we have to consuming them. This will mean paying the true value of what these goods are worth and paying the people who produce them a decent wage. And it will mean producing what we consume in a sustainable manner. There are solutions to these problems. Doing nothing because of any of these excuses is just a cop-out and it is what really distinguishes those who just talk the talk from those willing to walk the walk.

****

Example ii) In Response to the Same Basic Question

Every morning without fail I buy a bottle of water. This is the first item that compromises my ability to contribute to a more sustainable world. This is because of the amount of plastic that is used in bottling the water and how I just throw it in the bin most of the time without even recycling it. Not to mention the transportation impacts on the environment as well.

Even though I know that bottled water is a cause of unsustainability I continue to find myself making excuses to keep buying it. I always end up twisting my excuses to benefit my own self-interest without making myself feel guilty about it. For example, when I go to grab the bottle of water, for a few seconds I think about what I have been learning about environmental sustainability but then I find myself quickly snapping out of that and thinking about how I need it because I don't want to be thirsty or dehydrated in class because then I will have to stop and ask someone else for water and I wouldn't want to do that. I just want my own water. It always comes back to me and I make myself the number one priority to justify my excuses.

I also think to myself, well it will be fine, I will just get it this one time and after this I will buy a bottle I can refill with tap water. But this never happens and every day I continue to buy another bottle of water. I also tend to justify it with the clichéd excuse "I am only one person and one person alone cannot make a difference so I might as well buy it and not worry." I think that this thought has come somewhat from people telling me that I cannot make a difference and I totally believed them. Even my family, when I try and recycle plastic, cardboard etc. at home and try to emphasize the importance of recycling to them, they look at me as if I am a bit weird and taking things too seriously. My boyfriend even said to me "you alone cannot make a difference, there are millions of people in the world that don't even know let alone care about this stuff. What can you possibly do?" It really challenged me to think what can I do? In all honesty it is easier for me and a much more convenient option to sit back and "enjoy" the luxuries of my life than to sacrifice the little things and worry about the sustainability of our future. I always think someone else can look after that but who will? It made me think that if I am actually learning about the implications of these sorts of things on the wider world and the importance of making ethical decisions, yet I can still make these self-centered, selfish choices, what about the vast majority that don't learn about this and are ignorant of these issues?

When I talked to my sister about environmental sustainability she told me a story about when she went to the dairy and the shop-keeper was putting her milk in a plastic bag. She said she didn't need a bag and he said to her "You're not going to make a difference by not taking this one bag. People come in here and buy two bottles of milk and want a bag for each bottle, so you're not going to make a difference." I was disgusted when she told me this, but I can't say I am entirely shocked. This has become people's reaction to people like my sister who are trying to do little things to contribute to sustainability. They react like you are some kind of hippy or something. It really makes you think what's the point in even trying? Firstly, people look at me like I'm weird and secondly, they tell me I can't make a difference, so why bother trying?

I think that my excuses are totally invalid. I should realize that if I always let people tell me how to live my life I will never be able to make a change. I need to realize that even if no-one believes I can make a change or is willing to make a change, my own effort still counts. Maybe when the people around me see what I am doing it can encourage them to adopt the same thing. If I can put my words into action with passion I may influence others to do the same. I need to stop making excuses to serve my own self-interests. However, this is going to take a lot of will-power and is a lot easier said than done.

The second item that compromises my ability to contribute to a more equal or inclusive world is clothes. As ridiculous as it sounds, I do purchase at least one, if not two or sometimes three pieces of new clothing a week. This is partly because I work at a retail store and we always have to wear current season product that is not on sale, so I sometimes have to buy something new. And so the excuses start already—"I have to buy it for work." I also tend to buy new clothes from other stores as well, which are not justified. The others that I buy are pretty much always made in China. Most of these will come from sweat-shops where cheap labor or child labor may be used. This is a huge barrier to a more inclusive and equal world as many employees in sweat-shops are paid extremely low wages—most of the time not even enough to cover their daily needs so they continue to live in poverty. Furthermore, children who work in sweat-shops are often denied a proper education as they need to earn money to help provide for their families and don't get the chance to go to school. A lot of people are forced into these working conditions and trapped in a cycle of exploitation and inequality.

Even though I know this, I find myself buying impulsively and the excuses are endless. For example, I was at work on Saturday and on my lunch break I decided to have a look around the shops. I told myself that I would not buy anything but that did not work. I saw a really nice dress that would be perfect for my friend's 21st party that night. Again, just like the water situation, I had a debate with myself. I know where these clothes come from and the poor working conditions that are probably involved. But I hadn't seen the friends who were going to be at the 21st for years and I wanted to look nice and impress them with a really nice dress. After all, I have lost a little bit of weight and this could be my reward. That is what I told myself. I thought yes, I will get this dress and this will be my last buy. There was another excuse "my last buy." It is always my last buy, until I buy something else a few days later. I found myself making this same excuse a few days after when I went to the mall to have lunch. I walked past a swim-suit shop and thought I should buy a new bikini. I went onto the shop, looked at the tag which said "Made in China." I stopped for a second and thought about how this was probably made but I couldn't find myself really making the connection to care, as selfish and awful as that sounds. Again, I used the excuse that I had lost a little bit of weight and I deserved it.

My last example came about when I was at work on Saturday. I wanted to buy a top because the one I had was on sale. It would have been fine if I wore that top for the day and wore another top for the next time I came to work but instead I bought the new one. I told myself I have to buy this one because mine is on sale and I don't want people to think that I am breaking the rules and not wanting to wear the full price product. Plus, both of my colleagues were wearing full-price, new season product and I didn't want to be the odd one out. I was really just trying to find an excuse that wouldn't make me feel bad about buying some more clothes. It's just ridiculous, I don't need any more clothes. Again, it makes me think that if I know about where these clothes come from and under what conditions they are made and still continue to buy, what about the people who don't even look at the tag and don't know what is going on? What is ever going to change their minds about buying? Again, I feel that I am only one person and what difference can I really make? If no-one else is going to sacrifice their self-interest why should I?

Reflecting on all of this, I think why doesn't it influence me enough? Is it because I haven't actually seen the working conditions and really researched into it? Maybe I am not informed enough but that is still not a valid excuse. Ignorance is just trying to blame someone else. I made the choice to buy these clothes knowing that people may be denied life's needs so they can continue to make clothing for me to buy. I actually feel ashamed of myself.

Again, I feel that my excuses are extremely invalid. I am really ashamed of myself. I almost feel like Adrian Leftwich in the sense that I learn about environmental sustainability and ethical decision-making and I am quite happy to preach about it. Yet when it comes down to it, I crack under pressure. Not the same type of pressure that Adrian Leftwich had, but an internal pressure that leads me to making decisions that are the opposite to the way I present myself. I find that I end up tailoring the costs and benefits of an ethical decision to further my own self-interests. I feel like a hypocrite and in all honesty I really want to change this. I think it is going to take time and small steps and I truly believe that through the realizations of this reflection I have made the first step.

****

Example iii) Discrepancy and the Psychological Defenses Used to Maintain It

The essence of this assignment is to explain how my mind works in rationalizing my unsustainable and divisive consumption habits. From the start, even before thinking of anything I consume, I subconsciously start making excuses. "I can't think of anything…I am not a big part of the problem…I am not harming anyone…It's my choice…" These same thoughts continue throughout and represent the main excuses I use to justify my consumption habits. The excuses shadow the biggest excuse or justification that I use—ignorance. I simply turn a blind eye to the problem. I usually don't think about how my consumption impacts a sustainable and inclusive world. It seems my mind pre-empts the question and has the excuses ready. This makes answering the question hard as it seems to be solved before it begins!

After making a list of what I consumed over a couple of days, two goods stood out—my daily purchase of V (an energy drink) and the regular purchase of eye fillet steak. The former represents mindless and greedy consumption, with my demand spurring on processes that are unsustainable. The production of V (and other soft drinks) is unsustainable in its use of energy, water, transport, and the production of waste (particularly the packaging). My considerable daily demand for V directly compromises my ability to lead a sustainable life. The latter of these two goods, eye fillet steak compromises my ability to lead a more inclusive lifestyle. This particular cut of meat feeds into a sense of elitism and its high price represents a difference between the "haves" and the "have-nots." While part of the reason for the purchase is its taste, it has also created a reluctance in me to have "lesser" quality pieces of meat. The cut of meat may not be divisive per se, but the importance and status that my ego places on this consumption is.

Even as I write about these goods I can't stop myself from making excuses. I feel the need to diminish the link between the goods and the goals they compromise. I want to use language like "my consumption of V *might* be unsustainable" and "eye fillet steak *only sort of* feeds elitism." Distancing myself from the problems is a useful trick I use to make sure I can continue my consumption. It is just that though—*a trick*. Combined with this is my sense of not having *responsibility* because I am just a tiny consumer, one individual. Because the problem is so far removed and I am just one individual, I find myself thinking "Oh what's the point then…everyone else will keep drinking V so the demand will still be up and so will production."

I start thinking that to say my consumption of these goods compromises my ability to lead a sustainable and inclusive life is to infer a large dose of "but-for" causation. Such causation seems impossibly wide and unfair. The "for want of a nail" proverb captures my thoughts well.

For want of a nail, the shoe was lost
For want of a shoe, the horse was lost
For want of a horse, the rider was lost
For want of a rider, the battle was lost
For want of a battle, the kingdom was lost
And all for want of a horseshoe nail.

My mind creates the argument—is it really fair to say a purchase of V stops a sustainable world?

More specifically in relation to my consumption of eye fillet and inclusiveness, I find myself thinking that it is one of the least direct ways of creating a divisive world. Surely it is harmless and tiny compared with more obscene acts of consumption—like caviar or designer clothes. Those goods really create a sense of class division and people attach their egos to those goods. This feeds back into the justification that it is such a distant link from my acts to the goals of sustainability and inclusiveness. A distance so far in fact, that my tiny acts don't really stop the achievement of these goals.

The last justification I find myself coming up with once I have worked through all the rest is that consumption is a right I am entitled to. If it is my money, which I have earned, who is to say that I shouldn't buy another V or enjoy a good steak? As ridiculous as it sounds, I seem to link the freedom to consume wantonly to a basic human right.

At this stage I notice that a sense of anger has been brewing within me coupled with indignity and a sense of incredulousness. I almost want to yell "Who cares," "Why do I have to justify my consumption habits," "I don't have to justify myself to anyone." Again, amusingly and ridiculously, this "beast within" starts tying my justifications to other things— who am I as a person and what sort of character do I really have? It goes something like this: "If my consumption habits are so 'bad', am I a bad person? I have to be a bad person to have bad consumption habits. But I am not bad, I am good. Therefore my consumption habits can't possibly be bad." The logic of this is amusing in its absurdity but when coupled with angry emotions it is astonishingly powerful.

The above represents my unrestrained justification and the feelings that arise from the discrepancy between my ideals of a more sustainable and inclusive world and my consumption habits. I now turn to a more critical frame of mind to assess whether these justifications really stack up. The essence of my justifications is that I don't feel any responsibility for my consumption habits (for various reasons) and I stop myself from questioning this by ignorance and then an emotional reaction. When viewing my lack of responsibility it just doesn't stack up. I convince myself that I only play a tiny part and that others are worse and that I don't really impact negatively on achieving these goals. However, if I believe that mass change is necessary (which I do), then it is delusional to ignore the fact that mass change comes about by lots of individuals making their own small changes. A collective is merely made up of individual actions for a common purpose. My responsibility for personal change and to realize that I do form part of the wider collective is the same responsibility everyone else has. Even now I find myself arguing that some are more responsible than others, but in stepping back and viewing that thought, it may actually just be my ego trying to justify my habits again and shift responsibility to others. Essentially, when I tell myself there is a huge distance between my habits and stopping change coming about, I am trying to avoid my responsibilities. In linking the freedom to consume with the freedom of choice, I try and avoid my responsibilities. The reality is that I, as much as anyone else, am responsible for my action and for helping realize these goals.

The second method I find myself using to support my justifications is emotional. My ego ties my habits to who I am as a person meaning that if you question my habits, I get upset and view it as a personal attack. Of course, to link emotions with the discussion of bringing about change in this way seems silly. Twisting a discussion with emotions isn't a valid way to justify anything but it is a powerful way! Recognizing that it is not a valid method is easy—to stop using it as a support for my justifications is much harder. It forces you to really stop and ask why you are getting so wound up, why you are personalizing the discussion so much and seeing it as an attack on your character. For myself, such a reaction is most likely due to my ego basing who I am on how others perceive me. If I think that the question could be construed even slightly as an attack on who I hold myself to be, my ego automatically leaps to the defensive. The only real counter to this is to simply recognize it. Be realizing when I am heading down this path I can stop it and this justification for avoiding my negative habits will begin to fall away.

****

With just these three examples it is clear how readily broad themes begin to emerge in such writings as personal perspectives begin to overlap and converge. Dozens of such writings considered together contain a wealth of insight, and a central core of common, but also varying evasions. These create a solid foundation for identifying the essential patterns of denial that keep us all limited in responsibility and as these move into consciousness, they become identifiable and avoidable. Coming to recognize our defenses is a prerequisite for moving beyond them and in the above writings an unfolding of this potential is clearly present.

Reflective Writing on Challenging Inconsistency

Realizing how our own internal dialogue excuses irresponsibility can only be one part of learning though. It identifies the problem but it doesn't practice overcoming it. The next step in actualizing responsibility involves pushing ourselves to challenge these rationalizations and move from mere words to action. In so doing, we rouse the power of egotistical selfishness and see the real dynamics of resistance and resilience. Each of the following examples of student writing comes from attempting to exercise greater responsibility and reflecting on the experience of deliberate improvement.

Example iv) Restraining Consumption That Is Detrimental to Building a Better World

Challenging the Unconscious Consumer

The item that I have chosen to refrain from is make-up. Using make-up has been an everyday activity for me for the past twelve years. It is so embedded into my everyday routine that it was only when I asked my sister for assistance that she pointed it out—while I was bragging about how environmentally friendly I am and how this topic is not applicable to me. I know make-up products are not in themselves good for the environment, people or animals. In order to get a better understanding of this I had to do some research as I usually do not pay much attention to what happens in this industry. I do see the hypocrisy between my words and my actions. The following were the main impacts brought to light after a bit of research.

- Make-up is typically mass-produced in factories which would put a strain on resources and carbon emissions.
- The plastic used for packaging products is not bio-degradable and takes hundreds of years to break down.
- Almost 38,000 animals die each year because of product testing.
- The nano-particles that are present in a host of personal care products are extremely efficient in blocking out ultra-violet rays and exposure can lead to skin cancer. When these nano-particles get washed down the drains they find their way into the main water source of lakes, streams and rivers where they probably disturb the micro-ecosystem that maintains the marine environment.
- Every bottle of chemical-laden moisturizer threatens the marine environment as it disrupts the reproductive health of the fish population because of the presence of phthalates. Also a number of synthetic moisturizers are made from petrolatum which comes from petroleum, a non-renewable resource.

So it is evident that in order for me to feel "presentable and good" the damage to my bank-account is only a fraction of what the earth pays.

The Experience of Restraining Desire

For the whole week I had planned on not wearing any make-up at all. Before I actually started on my quest I expected the impact to be positive because it would mean I would get more sleep and some extra time in the morning so I could even have a real breakfast. And if I got a compliment it would be personally aimed at me, not at something I had deliberately created. As far as I was concerned, the application of make-up was so that I could present a better self to the world and I liked the feeling of comfort it gave me. It meant nothing more or less. But I ended up not even completing the challenge for a week.

On the first Monday morning, I got ready to leave for university, saw myself in the mirror and thought there is no way I can go out looking so "naked" and exposed to the world. I decided at this point that there is no harm in starting off slow and that tomorrow is better because I have fewer classes and fewer people will see me. So I applied some foundation and mascara. Throughout the day when I had guilty spells I justified my actions by telling myself that I already have the products; if I do not use them it will be a waste of money. I'm embarrassed to say that I even rationalized my actions by going as far as thinking that there are people out there that need me to buy these things in order to feed their kids and pay their mortgages and the world does not need any more unemployment.

It may seem that this was an oblivious reaction as it is drilled into our heads time and time again that people only wear make-up to hide behind a façade, to gain acceptance in society by making oneself look like the desired definition of beauty—and it all comes from our insecurities. Whenever these arguments have come up in the past, I have always defended myself and my decision to use an item by letting people know that it was a choice I made because I had the means and time to do so and then always went out of my way to convince people of the minimal amount I use. This really was a defense against what has now become the stereotypical view of those that choose to hide behind such a mask. It sounds a lot like drug-addiction. You never want to be one of the oblivious with a problem because you feel your situation is unique and an exception and it's impossible that you got sucked into the system.

The next day I gave my whole make-up collection to my sister and told her to hide it. So the next few days I stuck to my task. I got asked by my friends if I was ok because I did not look so well and was not as outgoing and happy as usual. I got asked by a complete stranger on the bus, and the ticket lady if I was ill. During these days I took these comments way too personally. I hated myself on the one hand because I felt I no longer blended in and stood out as this big ugly sick thing, but more importantly because I felt like an idiot for letting a bunch of face-paint have an impact on my outlook on life. I had an expectation that simply because this was the right thing to do, it would automatically have good consequences to an extent. Just so it is clear though, while I was sulking and feeling sorry for myself I was also very well aware just how superficial, clichéd and obvious this reliance and reaction was to the stereotype I was trying to avoid at all costs. At this point I had decided that it was all true. I cared about what society thought about me too much and because of this I was the way I was.

From how my days went I realize that as much as I want to blame society for creating my insecurities and "forcing" me to look a certain way it is just another justification for me to continue what I have always been doing. I woke up happy on the sixth day because in my office-based job hardly anyone would see me and those that do are like family to me so there would be no "societal expectation." Instead I got asked by a couple of the ladies who noticed my new look why I actually bothered with make-up as there was no need. It sounds like I was being influenced by a compliment I was desperately seeking here, but in its larger context this interaction was not to compliment me but rather to point out that I still looked good and seemed exactly the same. I went around and asked others' opinions and their reaction was the same. That night I went out to dinner with some friends, the same ones that told me I looked sick during the week without make-up, but with my usual self in tow. I ended up asking them at the end of the night if I looked different. They said they didn't really notice anything except I had less make-up on.

The biggest revelation for me was that I had unconsciously anticipated the reactions I had gotten in the first few days. In all of those days, it was not the make-up free face that anyone was concerned with, but rather my own emotional reaction to it as it was obvious that I was unhappy with it. I was so unhappy with it that it even had a physical impact on the way I dressed, moved and tried to disconnect myself from the world as much as possible. On the one hand I wanted it all to run smoothly, but on the other I was the one afraid of change. Society did not care too much one way or the other. I tried to blame the culture for not accepting me but really I went further than just make-up withdrawal and always related everything negative back to being deprived of it.

I went into this week with a lot of hope, absolutely hated it during the process but came out realizing that perhaps I need to stop over-analyzing and over-estimating the impacts of a positive change. The week went by and the next day I could make the choice to apply make-up or not, either way if I did it with good spirit no-one is concerned with how defined my cheek bones are. I have actually continued for the most part to go without make-up except on special occasions. I have in the process done a bit of research and will now definitely be purchasing products that are more eco-friendly and not tested on animals. I really hope that soon enough I will not need any at all but at this stage, I would be lying and in denial if I said that now, having gone for only two weeks of excluding most make-up from my life. But it has gone from being a part of the normal routine to something I think about before I actually use it and consider whether I actually need it. Before this exercise it was something I could not even differentiate from getting dressed. It is something I am sincerely going to continue.

It has also had an impact on other items of consumption. I no longer take plastic bags even if free, and I bought an eco-friendly water bottle to avoid purchasing plastic ones every day. I definitely have started paying more attention to what is contained in products and where they come from whereas once, it was only the purchase price that was the determining factor in my decisions.

Being more responsible overall definitely has had a very positive effect on me. I have always legitimized my actions by thinking the problem is too big and my just playing a small part in the destruction is not of any concern. It feels a lot better to not be a part of it.

****

Example v) Written in Response to the Same Challenge

In this reflective writing I have decided to change almost all of the cleaning products in my household to environmentally-friendly products. In the space of a week I have bought the following products: Laundry powder, multi-purpose surface cleaner, toilet cleaner, toilet paper, dish-washing powder, and hand-soap. I have decided to use the "Eco-Store" brand which is New Zealand made and strives to be environmentally friendly in as many ways as they possibly can. The reason I choose cleaning products was because they are something I use every day for several reasons. The idea came to mind when I wrote down the products I use on a daily basis and it made me realize I have a cleaning product in almost every room of the house. For example, I use a bench-cleaner in the kitchen after making meals, laundry powder for clothes washing, "spray n wipe" for other surfaces in the house, Jif and soap in the bathroom and obviously toilet paper and cleaner in the toilet. All of the products I used were not environmentally friendly and all contained harmful chemicals which are the underlying reasons why my previous consumption of these products works against the four values we say are most important.

Honesty—Firstly, I was being dishonest with myself. I was not taking the time and initiative to stand up for environmentally friendly products as much as I possibly could. It is simple to take a few extra minutes when shopping to look at what alternative products are available and are better for the environment. I feel now that I have started shopping for more eco-friendly products I am being more honest with myself and to my friends and family when I tell them what I have purchased and my reasons for it.

Compassion—Buying cleaning products which contain harmful chemicals is far from thinking and acting compassionately. And I agree that I am not taking enough care. I am very careful when it comes to disposing of rubbish and recycling so therefore I do not know what was stopping me from thinking more compassionately when it came to my consuming. My consuming eventually leads to disposing and this challenge has encouraged me to make a link between these two acts to try to make a difference.

Generosity—I clearly was not acting in a generous manner. I admit I was buying other cleaning products because they were the same ones my family used to buy when I lived at home and now that I am flatting, I just buy the same products out of habit. I would usually buy them when they were on sale which indicates I was thinking about saving my money when I should have been more concerned about the harmful chemicals I was putting in my shopping trolley. This challenge has encouraged me to look at the value of money and why I spend more on some things but less on others. I feel much better spending a few extra dollars on a product which I know will be safer for the environment. I feel being a little more generous in areas such as this is what I need to kick-start a positive mind and set about looking after the environment in as many ways as possible through what I buy.

Respect—I feel that now I am using safer products I am respecting myself as well as the environment. After doing some research I learned that there is no law for disclosing what ingredients are in cleaning products and some have not even been proven to be safe. By using these harmful chemicals I could have been putting myself at risk as well as the environment when I pour them down the drain.

My challenge was to go to the supermarket and look at what alternative products were available. This is where I found the Eco-Store products which catered to my needs in regard to this challenge. I have to admit I had never really looked at the packaging and marketing of these types of products. It was interesting to note that all the other products were in colored bottles and had attractive stickers and wording. The Eco-Store products are in white bottle with a very simple grey sticker. This goes to show I was clearly buying products that grabbed my attention and more than likely the ones that I liked the smell of. Admittedly this was the easiest part of the challenge. The hardest part was essentially justifying the price difference. There was a $2 to $5 difference for each cleaning item so I would be spending an extra $20 on cleaning products. However, now that I have taken on this challenge it is easy to think how long each item will last and I will only be replacing items as they became empty. The fewer times I go shopping for one is barely going to make a dent in the cost of my shopping. $2–5 is nothing. Also the Eco-Store products are concentrated so I am actually going to get more "bang for my buck." Why I made such a big deal about the money I am still debating with myself though. What's a few dollars here and there for the sake of the environment? Absolutely nothing when I would happily spend $10 on my house without blinking an eye. I also made the decision to buy the multi-purpose cleaner which saves two items that basically do the same thing. In another attempt to save money in certain areas of my life I purchased a re-usable coffee mug. I now use it every morning when I drive to university or work and do not need to buy coffee or tea. I was spending on average $17.50 a week on purchasing hot drinks from cafes, so this saves a little to justify spending more money on environmentally friendly products.

In saying this, I did need toilet paper and I almost subconsciously picked up the packet of Purex rolls which were on special at the supermarket. They were placed at the end of an aisle with a big yellow sign purposefully to get my attention. This was a bump in the road for my challenge. However, I was not going to give in so I walked to the toilet paper section and picked up the Earthcare rolls. By the time I got home and unpacked my shopping I was glad to have kept self-control and had already forgotten about the rolls which were on special. It is times like this where my thoughts will try to undo my best intentions. I will continue to challenge myself and most of all not be fooled by advertising or the marketing of products on "special."

To help encourage myself with this challenge, I thought it would be a good idea to have some moral support. I sent an e-mail to my close friends and family discussing this assignment and the underlying reasons for living more ethically. Of course I didn't put pressure on them to do the same but just explained what challenges I was going to make and invited them to join me if they liked. I mentioned about taking a few extra minutes to look at the products we're buying and see if there are better alternatives. It made me happy and proud to have shared my challenge with people close to me and I hope they might make a few changes to their everyday consuming as well. Sometimes it only takes one person to make a move in the right direction and others will be willing to follow. In addition to this, I thought of other ways to spread the rise of environmentally friendly cleaning products. In a generous act I bought an extra bottle of multi-purpose surface cleaner and donated it to the shopping bins behind the check-out. These bins donate the food and products to those who cannot afford them on their own.

I think it is important to note that I have researched the Eco-Store products which I am now using and have learned valuable lessons from this. "EcoStore" has a variety of scientists and chemists who continually evaluate their products and the impact on the health of people and the environment. They have an informative website which clearly outlines and discusses their philosophy and all the ingredients in their products. They use plant and mineral based products which are GE free, not tested on animals and are made with the utmost care and respect for the environment. One question I had was about the packaging and this was answered on their website. The plastic they use is a material called HDPE which is the most recyclable plastic currently available. Eco-Store has a long-term goal of setting up a system where their bottles can be re-ground and made into new Eco-Store bottles to be used again. They also have fully recyclable labels, laundry scoops, trigger sprays, 95% recycled laundry powder boxes and plan to remove the plastic bag in the laundry bags by July 2012. On top of all this, Eco-Store products are made in Auckland in the only factory in New Zealand to have a Diamond Enviromark to ensure all products are manufactured with the utmost care and consideration for the environment.

After reading all the information available on the Eco-Store website and completing my challenge of living more ethically I am 100% certain that I will continue to buy these products on a regular basis. I had read before this challenge that some environmentally friendly products were not as effective and required more elbow-grease but I have not encountered any problems and am very happy with their cleaning effectiveness. It has made me feel very fulfilled and I am proud to tell people about what I have achieved. Not only has buying more environmentally-friendly products been an ethical action for me but it has significantly prompted my thinking in many other areas of my daily life. I have been regularly using my re-usable coffee mug, told friends and family about the challenge and I recently booked a flight home and paid extra to off-set the carbon emissions from my flight. I have also set myself a new ethical challenge which is to begin using recyclable shopping bags and to buy a new drink bottle so I can reduce the number of plastic bottles I buy. On another note, I am going back to Thailand for a holiday next month. This will remind me of how other countries operate and how my views on ethical living have been significantly enhanced from taking this course. Though I have been to Asia many times I do feel that this trip may have a different effect on my thoughts and feeling. But I will take it in my stride as another learning curve about what changes I can make to my lifestyle for a better world.

****

Example vi) Same Question but a Different Outcome. (Note here the level of honesty applied when failing to uphold changed action for the assigned period).

A good which I consume more than anything on a daily basis would definitely be canned tuna. I eat a minimum of one can a day and a maximum of three. I am not the biggest meat eater as I don't like the taste. I eat chicken but not a lot of red meat so I compensate in eating tuna so I can get some iron into my diet. It is also high in protein, low in fat, and contains essential nutrients such as Omega-3. Not only for health reasons do I eat a lot of tuna, but it's very affordable and convenient and, of course, I love the taste. There are so many different ways you can eat it: In salad, with pasta, with stir-fry vegetables, by itself or with carrot/celery sticks. The list goes on.

There are lots of goods I consume on a daily basis which are affecting the sustainability of our future in some way. So why did I pick canned tuna? Well, something that alerted me to this issue was when I took my ten year old cousin to a science expo during the April school holidays this year. While looking around the expo we found ourselves at a marine stall which talked about the fisheries and what fish we should or shouldn't eat. Being a very intelligent ten year old, Kara quickly looked at the chart on display and pointed out the different fish to me. It is important to point out that she does not live in New Zealand, but was visiting for about a week and during that time had picked up that I eat a lot of tuna. Upon looking at the chart she said to me "Look, tuna is classified as one of the worst choices of fish and you eat a lot of tuna. Maybe you should stop or eat less." WOW. The guilt that I felt at that moment was intense. Even she noticed and understood the consequences of my actions. In all honesty, it was embarrassing to be told in front of a group of complete strangers that my level of consumption is damaging the future of not only tuna, but all fish and the ocean in its entirety.

In reply to her I was honest by acknowledging that yes, I do eat a lot of tuna and it was not a bad idea to decrease my consumption. But did I? No. Why, because right now I cannot see the direct impact it is having (because let's face it, it's all about me). I love the taste, it's good for my body and it is really difficult to change one's lifestyle unless I am willing to. However, I just knew that you were going to challenge us with a consumption experiment for a reflective writing piece, so in the back of my mind I thought I would try it anyway. And here I am. I already know what I am going to write because my ten year old cousin alerted me to my consumption behavior weeks ago.

One thing that motivates me for this challenge is the thought that my children and grandchildren may never be able to experience eating tuna. Pretty scary thought right? The most frightening aspect is that without a doubt it could happen. I don't want to be part of the generation that allowed this to happen. My consumption goes against hope for a better world because I am consuming at an unsustainable level. Not only is my rate of consuming concerning but I am also quite fussy when it comes to taste and I only eat Sealord tuna. After doing some research I found something that shocked me. I was reading information regarding fishing—I was on the Greenpeace site, when I discovered that Sealord tuna is caught unsustainably. "That's because Sealord gets its tuna from companies using the worst fishing methods—ones that catch endangered sharks, turtles, juvenile tuna and other sea creatures as well. These are known as by-catch and are often thrown back into the ocean injured, dead or dying. That's exploitation not expertise." That is pretty scary and after reading this, I decided that I would further challenge myself for another week. In this challenge I will eat another brand of canned tuna to see if I can actually eat it. Will my fussiness override the reality of the tuna's situation?

Taking all of this into consideration, I am going to challenge myself from today to not eat a single can or mouthful of tuna. This is going to be very hard for me as I don't independently go to the supermarket as I still live at home. In this respect it is going to be hard for me as tuna is always extremely accessible for me to eat. Therefore I am going to have to exercise self-control and independence in choosing what I eat. Before I started writing this reflective writing piece, little did I know that I had had my last tin of tuna for the week. This is going to change my diet, the number of cans my parents buy and how I think toward eating tuna. I know that in the back of my mind every time I want to eat tuna is my little cousin telling me that I eat too much and that it is damaging the ocean. If that's not motivation, then I don't know what is!!!??

It's been a struggle for me throughout this week not to eat tuna. It was always a quick fix when I was hungry. I had to stop myself when I went to the pantry for lunch, to constantly remind myself that I could not eat it. It didn't get easier, but it made me realize that we don't appreciate the simple ability and privilege of being able to eat tuna. I know that I take it for granted and it is this challenge that has caused me to reflect upon my attitude not only to tuna but to food in general. Because food is so accessible in my life, unless it's dinner when I typically stop to thank God for this food, I don't really stop to think about it—where it has come from, who has suffered, who is suffering, whose hands have labored to allow me to eat such amazing food. My lifestyle of busyness has caused me to be less appreciative of what I put in my body and my attitude demands food instantly, as a quick fix.

Futhermore, my observations of the dynamics of my own defenses, habits, and rationalizations show that they are compromising my integrity and values—so to answer that question, yes, they are. How? I have values to respect food, to respect how food is presented to me, the process it takes for food to arrive and all of this respect has gone out the window because of convenience. I now have this expectation that I can get anything healthy, delicious and quick. Eating tuna is so accessible that it has become an object, a thing to eat rather than something I respect and enjoy for the right reasons.

In responding to my second week of eating non-Sealord tuna, it was difficult because I find the taste so different. But by the end of it, it had become something that I could adjust to but it was definitely a mental framework that I had to push through. So now that I have challenged myself a week longer than asked, and in a different way, the big question is will I keep eating non-Sealord tuna? Honestly—No. Why? Because I don't really care that eating Sealord tuna is more unsustainable than other brands. As harsh as it is, I just don't care, and people don't care. We have society that is fixated on taking care of #1, which is ourselves and others are second to that.

Basically the future is looking very gloomy unless we act immediately and decisively. I know that just one person can make a difference, even if it as small as stopping eating canned tuna. However, in all honesty after this reflective writing will I stop? No. Tuna and chicken are basically all I eat with regards to meat, so I feel its ok as I don't eat excessive amounts of meat. Moreover, I don't currently see or experience a direct link to eating tuna to my life here in New Zealand. Isn't that statement too easy—too easy to write, too easy to say? I think that it is ignorant of me and downright lazy. I honestly recognize this and admit to it, but in relation to this situation, that is what I am.

And my little cousin? Was I too powerless to do anything? Or are there always going to be these issues? To be honest, I just don't care. I don't like this attitude about me though, because if I am demonstrating this toward her, what will she be like when she grows older? I want to set a good example for her but it's just too hard. I guess I feel ok about it because it doesn't seem as bad as doing drugs, abusing alcohol, rebelling against my family or sleeping around. But to her it means something. Wouldn't it just be awesome if the little things like that also meant something to us older people who actually determine the future because what we do sends a message to the rising generation that it is okay. But we have to remember that just because people before us acted in a certain way, doesn't necessarily make it right. We are a society that has developed a "copy cat" notion where we see people partaking in it, we think we can do the same. Our own habits and rationalizations have impacted our ideals and our selfishness. Our careless nature and unwilling attitude to care have put our ecosystems in jeopardy.

****

These examples again illustrate the richness of discussion and the constant realization of how complex the challenge of enacting greater responsibility in our lives really is. The results of trying to harmonize ideals with action vary with most admirably rising to the challenge. But some, like the last example, find the challenge too overpowering. Taken together and across many more varied answers they bring to the fore many immediate emergent issues—including the question of why some care enough to resist self-defined irresponsibility while others don't. What is going on here? Such emergent findings can easily and immediately be thrown back to the class to reflect on.

Reflective Writing on Practicing Kindness and Generosity

As outlined when discussing the flow of the core questions that structure a course in educating *for* responsibility, challenging restriction is again, only a part of realizing a greater responsibility. Of ultimate importance in building a resilient responsibility is the appreciation that doing good really does feel good and that finding harmony between one's ideals and actions is fundamentally humanizing and ennobling. The writings in this final section are in broad response to challenges to put more generous, kind or appreciative modes of behavior into practice and reflect on the experience.

Example vii) Being Challenged to Perform an Act of Generosity and to Reflect upon the Dynamics Involved

The Irony of Generosity

Before I could undertake a generous act, I first had to think hard about what it was that I could do. I ran through all of the options in my head from cooking dinner for my constantly on-the-go mum who never has a moment to stop, to simply picking up the litter around my neighborhood. And then it struck me, the realization that I wanted to do something that would make a real difference to somebody—something they would remember for a long time. It turned out that something I saw on television a few weeks ago made my mind up as to what to do.

A family friend of ours has a little girl, Emily (name changed) who has Asperger syndrome. I decided to use this as the basis of my generous act. I thought long and hard about how I could incorporate Emily into the task assigned as there were so many complications surrounding it. I couldn't really take her out for the day as she really needed to be in the comfort of her own home surrounded by familiarity. I couldn't do anything that would intrude too much on her routines which made it very difficult to find a solution. Finally I decided that I would break it down to the most simple option and just look after her—just be with her for an entire day so that her parents could go out and do the things they needed to without the added stress of worrying about Emily. It doesn't sound like much of a luxury but to them it was a concept almost unheard of in the past four and a half years! I phoned up her mother and put to her my idea for their Saturday… and after a little bit of hesitation she decided to give it a go.

Before embarking on my day with Emily I have to admit that I was nervous beyond belief. The stories I had heard in the past about children with Autism and Asperger's and the info I had read on the internet in order to prepare myself, had me incredibly worried about what I had gotten myself into. A few times I tried to get my mum to join me as I was completely out of my comfort zone and for a moment I thought that I had chosen an act of generosity that was beyond my capability. The previous night I had sat myself down in front of my laptop, opened up Google and typed "things to do with a child with Asperger Syndrome." I found out that unlike children on the Autism spectrum, children with Asperger are not usually withdrawn around others—they will approach people even if somewhat awkwardly. Well there go my hopes of banging out a marketing assignment while there. And there it was—I had already stumbled across selfishness taking over from my generous act. Was I really sitting there hoping this kid was autistic so they would stick to themselves and leave me to make a move on an assignment? I was shocked that that was my first reaction.

On my way to their house I was hashing out how I would approach the day. At every red light I would pick up my printed pages of "How to pick activities for Asperger children" and "Babysitting guides for children with Asperger Syndrome." No-one could say that I was under-prepared for this day! However, as I sat with all these printouts in my lap, I still had this anxiety building up inside me and was incredibly close to turning around a few times. I stopped to buy coffee on the way so as to procrastinate about the situation, even if only for a few minutes. As I stood in line I was thinking "*good thinking, this will calm you down. Why am I working myself up so much? She is just a child.. and you have met here half a dozen times—will this time really be so different?*" I jumped in the car, put all my notes in the back seat and flicked on the radio in an attempt to drown out all the chaos in my head and off I went. I made the call that in order to work and be successful, I needed to clear my head.

Once I got there her parents opened the door and knew instantly that I had been stressing out way too much so they gave me a quick run-down. They said Emily usually sticks to diet she is used to and we have sorted her lunch for you. All you have to do is heat it up. She has had breakfast and we will be back by dinner. They said they would appreciate it if I didn't take her out and about—just because that could get a bit difficult for me. Her mum then stopped and said "Don't worry, it won't be nearly as hard as you've built it up to be." Then they showed me to where Emily was playing.

I have been asked to describe what I felt during conducting this generous act but to be honest, I didn't even have time to think about how I felt. Emily had me jumping from one activity to the next. We played outside on the swings, spent time organizing her toys and then watched a video her parents had approved. However, she spent the entire movie asking questions about what was happening. To my surprise she wanted me to be involved in everything she was doing. I guess this made me feel quite silly as I had hyped myself up so much and in reality it turned out to be quite fun. I felt very chuffed with myself. I could see how doing the simplest act of conducting weekend errands could become quite stressful for her parents and would take much longer than usual with Emily tagging along. As I began to feel happy about what I was doing for the family, I began thinking that if this is what it feels like to carry out a generous act why don't more people do it? If it is purely for the benefit of somebody else, why is it making me so happy? People need to stop thinking that doing something good has no benefit for you at all as it clearly does. Maybe not in an easily tangible sense, but the overall feeling you receive definitely outweighs the time lost carrying it out. As my mind began to wonder, trying to answer these questions I felt the garage door opening through the floor.

To my surprise her parents were back by 3pm. My 5 hours had flown past and it had not been nearly as difficult as I had anticipated. However, I was absolutely knackered! She had really taken it out of me—but it wasn't as hard as I thought it would be with nothing to do in a situation smothered by awkward moments. It was definitely hard work though in the sense that for those 5 hours I don't think I stopped for long enough to think about or reflect on what I was doing. It was go, go, go.

While driving home I found more time to reflect on the situation. I was really quite angry and it took me a long time to figure out why. It was only after a long conversation with my mum when I got home that I figured out the source of my anger. It came from the show that had set all of this in motion. The show was about educating the public on the fact that in New Zealand there is very little help or aid around for parents with children on the Asperger's spectrum and nothing like there is in Australia. If I was as exhausted as I was simply from 5 hours with Emily, what about all those other families dealing with children farther along the spectrum? Where was all the help for them? Once I had dealt with the anger and disappointment toward the government for this, I felt very satisfied with myself. I too had learned an awful lot about the syndrome and it has sparked the desire to do more to help children living with these syndromes. Not to mention that Emily's parents were very grateful and appreciative for allowing them to do something as simple as completing some weekend errands.

What was most ironic about the whole situation though is that because I was already friends with the family (the parents more so) I don't think that it has had too much impact on our relationship. The person it has had most impact on was me. Considering that this was meant to be an act of generosity purely for someone else's benefit, I do find it most ironic that it was me in the long run that it has helped the most.

****

Example viii) Exercising Kindness in a Series of Actions over Several Days

Acting with Kindness

I struggled with how to start these acts of kindness and where to start them. Who do I really help and how? What can I do for others that would make their lives easier? I decided to start close to home at my flat. I knew that some of my flat-mates had been swamped with university assignments and would not have a chance to cook themselves a decent healthy dinner. I thought I would scrape my ingredients together and buy a few extra things from the supermarket and make a roast for us to share. I was very excited because I knew that everyone was in need of some time to sit down and relax and enjoy a meal together.

My flat-mates were confused and shocked. They initially asked me how much money they owed me in return for the ingredients. I told them it was covered but could tell that they struggled with this as they are used to eating separately. I could tell though that they all deeply appreciated it.

That afternoon I dropped into work to drop off some work equipment that needed to be returned. I could tell a few staff members from other departments had a lot of deadlines to meet. I didn't have much to do that day so I offered to stay around and help them get a few things done for a couple of hours. I understood the stresses of working in the office and wanted to help my distant workmates as much as possible so I spent the afternoon helping one of my colleagues on a few projects she has happening in the community. She was very grateful for my help although she asked me how I could record these extra hours so I could get paid. I was surprised at this as I was not expecting to get paid. It was simply my task of helping another in a common environment. I could see how she thought pay incentives were the answer for my additional hours at work, but I assured her that it was fine and that I wasn't helping her in order to receive any additional payment.

On the second day I decided to help a neighbor out. She had been renovating the front of her house and there was garbage everywhere. I thought I would pop over when the builders were there and clean up the rubbish to help her out as she has several young kinds to look after. As I was cleaning she came out and expressed how thankful she was for my help. I do not have close friends with young children and her sincere thanks allowed me to see how time consuming and challenging being a parent is to young children. I felt really good about helping her out. This act of kindness allowed me to get to know my neighbor better but what I feel best about was that she knew she had kind neighbors concerned about her situation.

On the same day I bought a stranger coffee. This came about quite by accident. I was at a café and the person in line ordered a coffee and realized that they didn't have their money card to pay for it. This was a very small act of kindness but I felt equally good about helping the individual out. He was extremely surprised that I would help him out when I didn't even know his name. The coffee was only a few dollars and was in the process of being made. In the scheme of things, buying a coffee for a stranger is no big deal. But I noticed that it was a big deal for him that I would help in such a small matter. That became of interest to me, the different way we both saw things.

On my final day I wanted to help my flat-mate out. She has been extremely busy at university so I thought I would help her out by doing a few loads of washing for her. This again was a small task but I knew that cleaning up her room would put her in a cleared head-space and help her with her studies. I felt great about doing this and she was very pleased. I could tell a weight was lifted from her shoulders as she too knew she had a support system that could help when it was needed.

On the final day I thought of someone who means a lot to me, who has done a lot for me and who would really appreciate an act of kindness. I thought about my grandparents who live in the South Island and who I barely make enough time to see. I wanted to send them something small that they would appreciate over the winter months. I found some warm socks that I knew would help their circulation and that they would use. My grandparents rang me a few days later and were so pleased. They mentioned that they don't usually receive gifts from their grandchildren and were very appreciative that I had them in mind. I felt immediately guilty that I had not taken the time to do such simple, kind things as ring them regularly to see how they were. Their reaction to such a simple gift made me realize how much they appreciated the small kindness.

I was, and still am very surprised at the outcomes felt from these acts of kindness and compassion. I feel as though people are scared or frightened of generosity because it takes away an individual's attention on themselves and their own resources. However, I feel that the outcomes I felt demonstrate the opposite. I feel that I gained so much satisfaction from these simple acts of kindness. The reactions I received made me feel as though it was normal for friendship and communities to run off selfishness, greed and mistrust and that acts of kindness are something out of the ordinary. This realization is extremely disappointing. Not because I didn't get the reaction from people that I wanted, but more because I learned more about human behavior and how much we have become cold, untrusting and focused on our own needs and not others. We assume that any kind act must be met with some monetary reward to make it worth pursuing.

The positive sensations that I felt from the actions has made me want to continue engaging them as regularly as possible. One reason for this is that I feel that you alone can gain so much from assisting another. In my circumstances I felt that by giving only a small amount of attention to others needs I was able to strengthen my relationship with friends, family and others in the community. I think people have forgotten how generosity can be seen as a circle, not a direct line, implying not that you will receive some favor because you helped someone else directly, but more because of the emotional shifts that can occur—the bonds that grow, the trust that people give back to you as a member of a broader community.

Ultimately this exercise has led me to see how rare acts of pure generosity are. I view this as a wake-up call in the sense that it has showed me how urgently society needs individuals who are willing to act with compassion and generosity to benefit others. Otherwise, communities will continue to grow further apart and be run on greed, dishonesty and disrespect—things that promote a more negative world. I hope that small acts of kindness like those demonstrated earlier will help restore peoples' faith in human behavior and that this relationship will encourage others to act with more compassion and kindness to promote a better world.

****

To end with, a sample of writing that takes us back to the start and an exercise on raising money for famine relief. It is a good example to end with as it demonstrates the remarkable potential for responsible action that lies just below the surface in every class of young people. This responsibility extends to self-directing action beyond the parameters set. It demonstrates an extending, broadening, and deepening understanding of what responsibility requires, and a capacity to act in the name of a more harmonious thriving. This is the fitting end-point toward which all of these reflective writings aim.

This example was written in response to asking the group to engage in a money-raising exercise (asking three people they knew to give $5 for famine relief in the Horn of Africa). The challenge was set in response to uncovering a powerful sense of collective futility and distance in previous writings—about why the group consumed irresponsibly. I wanted to challenge this feeling by having the group as a whole raise some money to give to Oxfam and to have representatives come to collect the money, explain how it would be used and thank them—all in the hope that they might feel more empowered to make a difference. As explained in the example that opened this section, the assignment began by asking learners to watch some YouTube footage of the unfolding famine to exercise compassion.

Example ix) Challenging Feelings of Futility and Distance

The purpose of this exercise and the subsequent reflection was to put ethics into practice acting on the attributes personally needed to create a better world. Personally, it also turned into an exercise of rationalizing against the methods of the ego. I found that emotions and rationality are tools used by both "sides" of one's self.

In the previous reflection I highlighted how anger was used by my ego to justify the excuses used to continue my bad habits. This time other emotional methods were employed when watching You Tube clips on the Horn of Africa. This time, instead of anger I found my ego using emotions such as despair, helplessness and futility. My response almost straight away was that it was too much, too sad, too far-gone to help and that I couldn't help anyway. At the same time I felt as if I had seen it all before, that it wasn't real in a sense. I could somehow detach what they were going through from any form of reality.

As these feelings washed over me I had to stop. Why was I feeling so helpless and detached from their suffering? Also, how had I somehow de-sensitized myself to it? One explanation would be the amount of violence, pain and suffering that I've seen in movies and games. Maybe those experiences had prepared my ego to automatically detach and distance suffering in case I was overwhelmed by their pain i.e. as a defense mechanism. But this explanation might also be a cover for more selfish motives for not connecting with others' suffering. Could it be that I was feeling emotions that would result in distancing myself from their suffering— because of more nefarious reasons? Laziness, greed and selfishness come to mind as attributes my ego would be trying to promote rather than empathy. The rationale being "If I was empathetic I would have to do something to help; If I had to do something to help, I might be forced outside my comfort zone—I might be forced outside my routine."

Realizing this made me think that I couldn't let it go on—it couldn't be my response to what I was watching. It seems appropriate to bring to light some other emotions that were running through me. Seeing video of skeletal children, large eyes in sunken faces, you would have to be inhuman not to care, not to feel their pain and see their suffering. I did care. I do care. It wasn't a problem about feeling empathetic, rather it was that this was being overwhelmed by other emotions being thrown at me by my ego.

It made me think that just as rationalizing excuses can make them more powerful, rationality was also just a method to be used. It could work for the ego or against it. It dawned on me that in order to play down the emotions put forward by the ego, I would need to support the more promising emotions I was feeling. On reflection, it seems clear to me that both emotional responses and the process of rationalizing are tools, methods to be used. It really just depends on which way they are put to use—either to create a better world and put ideals into action, or to maintain the status quo and remain insulated in one's own world.

Approaching Three People for Donations

With this strength of conviction I turned to the second task, to approach three people and ask if they would also donate to the cause. It was here that I changed tack from the set assignment. I knew of three friends instantly who would be responsive. It wouldn't be a personal challenge to ask them. I wouldn't be put out of my comfort zone and I wouldn't really be testing my ethics in practice. Nor would their emotional responses be unexpected. However, as I have been programmed to complete assignments as instructed, I did ask three people. Their emotional responses were as predicted. "Horrible," "tragic" and "devastating" were comments repeated when the suffering was outlined. Two of the three willingly gave well more than the $5 suggested. None seemed to even contemplate that they wouldn't help. The value of surrounding yourself with friends who also have the same ideals is amazing for strengthening one's integrity—the importance of friendship is a theme that runs throughout this reflection.

As indicated before, I didn't really feel I had tested myself as the exercise required. A friend, Maya (name changed) also felt the same thing. We thought that if the goal is to put ethics into practice and see our emotional responses, why not try a bit more? Being Law students we thought why not approach the Law School? Could we rally the student body down there to help? It didn't take much to come up with a plan for a fund-raiser outside the Law library. Putting this into action provided a much more rewarding experience in terms of understanding myself and my responses to other peoples' suffering and gave me a broader picture of others' responses as well.

The plan grew quickly; we would set up a stall outside the library with posters outlining what was happening and invite people to donate. We'd use social networking to good use—the Facebook event we set up (Bringing the Law School Love to Africa) reaching about 350 people. Maya thought of giving away some baking too, as a little thank-you from us. We had a spontaneous offer from a random person of baking, which was incredibly motivating for me. It was encouraging that someone that we didn't know wanted to help and would put the time in to make and bring some baking. This tiny, generous act had a huge impact on my commitment and was inspiring. Some would argue that, despairingly, people are too insulated in their own lives—especially apathetic students. While true on some level, this exercise really highlighted that, to me, people do care and are inherently part of a collective.

My feelings in the build-up to the event were mixed. I felt nervous about the event—would it succeed, would I be embarrassed, would it fail miserably?. I went to the printers and got 6 A3 posters printed the day before the event—still questioning whether it would work and whether I would just end up disappointed. I almost wanted to call it off. It would be much easier to stick with just asking three people, I wouldn't have to put myself "out there" so much and it would be less hassle. My ego was working in overdrive to stop me. But we did do it and it was awesome.

On the day of the event we set up at 9am. Our approach was that we didn't want to hassle people and we didn't want to guilt-trip people. Rather we wanted to be passive and let whatever happens happen. This way we could raise money and observe the reactions of people. While setting up, a few people asked what we were doing and I found myself happy, driven again. The doubt about the event that had crept into my mind disappeared and before I knew it lots of people were coming past and donating. We didn't need to push people. The most rewarding thing was to see people walk past, go to study and then come back out later just to drop some money off—it just seemed that they were particularly struck by the appeal and went out of their way to give. Clearly they empathized with the people in the Horn of Africa. The amount that people gave was awesome to see. Students obviously live on a budget, yet we had lots of

$10 and $20 notes going in. While a lot gave their spare change, it was obvious that the will to give and to care was there. We'd thank each person who gave and a lot of these people turned it around and thanked us. This sat uncomfortably with me but at the same time it was nice. Maybe it was pleasing because it stroked my ego to have the recognition, but it seemed to me that they were the generous ones and that we were merely facilitating it.

What could be termed a second "type" of donators was also evident. Some people approached it as if they were buying the baking. To me it seemed as if they had to convince themselves that they were getting something material and tangible in return, making it like a normal purchase. While the donations they gave were far in excess of the cost of a muffin, I wonder whether it was a rationale that they used to justify donating. While it didn't detract from their generosity, it underscored (in my opinion) how different people are at different places with themselves, their egos and their empathy.

The last group I observed were those that didn't give, or gave when they didn't want to. I say this not in a judgmental way, but rather to highlight the different levels of peoples' control over their egos and excuses. What struck me was that people who donated, and it would come up in conversation that they still thought it was futile, that "it was just another famine in Africa, again." They obviously cared because they donated, yet the excuses that we use to justify our negative actions were overtly present, specifically the futility excuse. To me this futility disappeared as soon as we started collecting significantly more and more money. While I couldn't donate much on my own, drawing on the resources Maya and I had at the law school—the network of friends and associates—proved that together we could do something. This fed back to feelings of satisfaction for me as Maya and I had facilitated this group action.

The determination and drive that filled me did wane at various times during the day. I ended up sitting there for 6 hours and at times I thought I should be doing other assignments that were due soon and at times it was uncomfortably cold. But we were resolved to stick it out for the day, an extra hour could bring in that little bit more. The reward came when we counted up the money, over $400 raised! It struck me that we could make a huge difference. The emotions that my ego had raised when watching the You Tube clips were well and truly beaten back. Rationalizing and supporting the more promising emotions such as empathy was worth it. I felt elated. The day spent away from doing work was not a loss, rather it was one of the most satisfying days I've had in a long while. I felt like I was giving my time and effort to something more worthwhile, something meaningful. It felt nice to be beyond my own little world and be part of a collective. It felt awesome seeing the response from the Law School—other people were reaching out of their worlds as well.

When looking at the class total (over $2,300 dollars raised by a class of 50), the same thoughts struck me—we can help, we can make a difference. More fundamentally for me however was that I had seen people become part of this collective, people reaching out for others. It gives so much promise to creating a better future. People get caught in despair about how greedy and selfish people have become, but down at the Law School that day I experienced the opposite. For me, it is this positive collective consciousness that will enable the creation of a better world. I believe that people are inherently good, it's just that the ego can overshadow this sometimes. It was heartwarming to see my faith in people confirmed.

CHAPTER 4

The Broader Context of Educating *for* Responsibility

- Assessment in Educating *for* Responsibility
- Resourcing and Lecturing *for* Responsibility
- Resourcing and Lecturing in Educating *for* Responsibility
- Applying Educating *for* Responsibility in Other Contexts

The principle of education should be creating men and women who are capable of doing new things, not simply repeating what others have done.

Jean Piaget

Tell me and I'll forget; show me and I might remember; involve me and I'll understand.

Chinese proverb

Assessment in Educating *for* Responsibility

The sample writings above illustrate some of the dynamic and multi-layered learning that students achieve while working to the various reflective writing briefs. These represent the primary measurable indices of how much is being learned but they can be usefully complemented by integrating assessments of factual learning and group work to extend the range of judgment. The many other forms of subsidiary learning that students develop including their abilities to negotiate perspective, find common ground, listen, and compromise are less amenable to measurement but absolutely critical to responsible empowerment. These supporting skills emerge organically in a collaborative process and can be left to develop on their own as students debate and integrate perspective in small groups. In any case, these are involved invisibly in the quality of reflective writings as these are inevitably informed by attending to others views and working constantly to incorporate them. Integrative reflective writings that balance form with freedom allow learners to demonstrate complex and uniquely individual understandings in ways that more constrained assessments deny.

There are a selection of reflective writing assignments in Appendix I which illustrate how these are explained to students and the detailed guidelines for writing they contain. High quality work begins with good instructions, and in prompting reflective expression, assignments have to balance structure with openness so that what is required is clear but within that, there is much latitude for individual initiative and expression. In the case of asking learners to practice more generous action for instance, the need to push beyond limits is a requirement but the choice of specific action is left to the learner. Written in this way, a great diversity of insight can be generated by a group in ways that are usefully focused and highly amenable to essential summary.

Reflective writings are generally written to accompany each of the five core themes involved in educating *for* responsibility and through this, attention and effort are efficiently focused on the key prerequisites for responsible action. Through these exercises learners work to define the future they want, discern the responsible means to it, explain the compromises they engage and explore the dynamics of acting more responsibly. Writing reflectively on these themes means that time and careful attention are given to questions of fundamental importance. This assessed work is closely woven into the fabric of the larger process though, as each aims to deepen and extend an ongoing learning in the broader context of the course. The collective conclusions of each reflective writing create the structural content that gives form to educating *for* responsibility. Thus, the nature of a better world, the core values needed to get there, the main barriers to progress and so forth, are all consolidated through reflective work.

These writings provide the primary measurable outputs for assessment but the diverse qualitative improvements that are revealed do not fit easily within the convenient marking schedules of education as usual. In education as usual students are tested primarily on the retention of factual knowledge which makes assessment relatively easy. Answers tend to be either right or wrong and those many students who want to know exactly "where marks were lost" can be shown specifically where points were deducted for incorrect or incomplete answers. It is understandable that even a few robust demands to justify marks by students lead many teachers towards a minutely quantified rigidity in assessment, but it is also deeply regrettable. At its nadir, these pressures produce courses in which assessment becomes the only meaningful end, killing broader exploration and limiting learning to only those things that 'will be on the exam'.

In educating *for* responsibility assessment is not an end, but a means to further learning. It cultivates deep integrative thinking about the self, its processes, and its relation to a larger world of responsibility. Attainment on these dimensions cannot be meaningfully measured by any rigidly quantifiable rubric. Rather, as the learning outcomes involved are organic and holistic, they demand a means of assessing that is correspondingly organic and holistic. This creates a challenge for educators as it calls for a more varied and subtle range of skills to be employed in accurately evaluating learners' progress. The deepest challenge for both students and teachers comes with the impossibility of developing a rigid rubric that assigns quantitative marks for making specific points. Given the freedom that exists within the broad form of each reflective question, answers are hugely diverse and accord to no simple ideal form. This is useful in allowing learners to express themselves genuinely and in generating diverse insights to work with, but it means that evaluations have to be more global and fundamental than is usual. The assessment of learning has to consider work as an integral whole and gauge the sincerity of effort, the depth of reflection, the breadth of thinking and the level of integration among other criteria. These indicate how active learning is for each student and are qualitatively robust and readily apparent when working in this mode.

The greatest insight into how reflective work is assessed in practice can be gained by looking at the sample feedback documents in Appendix II. These documents explain how reflective work was qualitatively assessed and demonstrate how the criteria for excellent, good, and poor work were applied. As in all reflective work, the central criteria discussed (as also in the assignment outlines) are engagement, deep reflection, and integrative thinking. To some these may appear to be rather unquantifiable but in application they are easy to work with and easy to defend as legitimate and accurate ways of gauging learning. It is true that grading qualitative work takes some practice and it is perhaps advisable that anyone considering a move to this form of teaching begin with one or two assessed exercises. However, it does not take long to acclimatize and make robust qualitative distinctions that can be communicated clearly and justifiably. In surveying the sample assignments in Appendix I it will be clear that these call for a certain level of maturity from learners as they ask them to move beyond a dependence on minute direction. Most are more than ready for this and I find that students generally respond maturely and indeed appreciate a more qualitative and holistic framework for assessment.

The collaborative nature of educating *for* responsibility encourages a considerable broadening and deepening of perspective and the potential for transformative learning is considerable. Indeed many students refer to the experience as genuinely life-changing. Given the opportunities to learn, young people can be, and should be, held to very high standards. It is important that learners be stretched in all dimensions and pulled beyond the inertial limits of habitual thought and action. It is important that they be genuinely challenged and assessing work on the degree to which they rise to the challenges set in a spirit of deep enquiry is entirely appropriate. It means that at the start at least, many will be assessed qualitatively and numerically as "could do much better"—a designation understood and accepted by almost all. Where learners do not do well in assessment it is generally due to a lack of effort rather than ability and this is a key point to make in providing feedback. I tell all groups that I have endless respect for their potential but that it would be insulting to both them and to me if I were to give high marks for work that falls short of what they are really capable of. Learning to do better is helped enormously by the feedback documents that accompany the return of assessed work and also by the personally tailored feedback that can be given on individual papers. Providing samples of good work also helps learners appreciate how their own work may have fallen well short of what was possible. This is valuable practice not only in this regard but also in order that learners get to read some of the most interesting work being produced by their peers.

Any early assessment concerns can be somewhat allayed by giving learners the opportunity to find their feet in what is for many a completely new form of expression. Depending on the institution, many learners may have had no previous opportunity to express themselves in such a thoughtfully independent manner. In assigning a number of reflective writings I usually allow the poorest grade for each student to be dropped—meaning that if there were five reflective writings required, only the best four marks would count towards the learner's final grade. An alternative way of making people more comfortable with this unfamiliar form of writing is to allow failing assignments to be resubmitted. This is particularly useful at the start of a course where some might find the change of mode difficult, or not fully trust that personal expression is what is actually required.

As engagement grows and learning in the broader context of the course becomes more focused, the quality of work tends to increase across the board, pulled by demanding standards. Submissions are generally of a very high quality and this allows learning to be expressed and rewarded meaning that in educating *for* responsibility, more students can receive good grades than is usually the case. I have little time for the bureaucratic insistence that a rigidly "normal" grade distribution be forced on learners—preordaining failure for a significant number and mediocrity for the majority. A successful education should see many more achieving excellence than this. Education and all its component parts should make exceptional learning attainable for as many as possible and this is what this emergent and collaborative approach is designed to do. The reflective writings that lie at the heart of assessment allow students to demonstrate an expanding capacity for responsible thought and action and this is complemented by two other subsidiary means of rewarding constructive learning.

Other Assessments

Educating *for* responsibility involves not only learning to reflect and articulate a personal perspective, but also an extensive coverage of a variety of informative media relating to the topic and useful for expanding horizons. The details of what materials might be useful in this regard are covered briefly in the next section, but in the context of assessing learning a few comments are appropriate. If good resources are drawn from a wide variety of sources, learners' horizons can be expanded endlessly. Although I try to develop as intriguing and enlightening a body of resources as possible so that most engage willingly, there are always some in any group who will require a bit of a "stick" to keep up with resources. One way of dealing with this is to give a series of unpredictable short tests in class covering materials that should have been read or watched in the last two weeks. These are 10-minute short-answer or even multiple-choice tests that efficiently assess whether learners are covering the core materials set for study or not. The efficiency of these is greatly enhanced by having learners take these short tests in class and mark each other's papers. This is a simple process that involves giving the anwers verbally immediately after the test is taken and having class members total the score for an anonymous peer. In this way feedback is immediate and a great deal of dead marking time is saved. Quick, unannounced "on-the-spot" tests are not only a good way of ensuring that people are doing the background learning, it also rewards those who are fully engaged and increases attendance as no one except the teacher knows when a test might suddenly appear.

A second easily applicable component of assessment involves group work. One variation that is very useful in practice is that of designing a progressive business to facilitate the better world learners wish to see eventuate. Working on such a project should begin early in the semester (as soon as the criteria for effective action are articulated) in order to allow time for developing these innovations. Group work is often challenging for learners and there is often some resistance to breaking out of the prevailing mode of working alone. Given the high level of the challenge set though, it is very useful to have learners combine their insights and divide energies across a range of tasks. The biggest complaints from students in group work tend to involve difficulties in dealing with "free riders" and finding time to meet. These are legitimate concerns but not insurmountable ones. With regard to finding times for groups of around six to meet, it is easy to make available class time for working on the project when all can be there, and are there. Beyond this, there are creative online means of working together including Wikispaces where documents can be worked on collaboratively by different members at different times and different places. With regard to "free-riding," groups can be reminded that team work is likely to be a big part of their future and that it calls for interpersonal skills to ensure that a fair share of work is put in by all. As part of an education *for* responsibility, all groups should be challenged to manage their own affairs in a responsible and constructive way without the need for an outside authority to intervene.

As outcomes for assessment, groups can be challenged to produce written business plans, videos and presentations in order to sell their innovations to their peers. Given that projects are working to the vision of a better world created by the class as a whole, it is appropriate to involve the class in judging whether an idea is progressive or not. In one variation, teams can be asked to present their business ideas for a better world to the class for its evaluation. Each team involved can be given a thousand dollars of play money to invest in up to five ideas (excluding their own). The money is divided up (good to give lots of small value notes) and awarded to those teams with the ideas judged most worthy of investment. Apart from being a fun and active process, the deliberations over which ideas are the worthiest (and why) range far and wide as learners actively think about whether the ideas would really contribute to building a better world and how. At the end of the process, grades are assigned in part by the amount of investment money raised from their peers. Student evaluations can count for half of the final team grade with the other half being the teacher's evaluation. Alternatively, external guests or a panel of judges might assess projects. The specifics of assessment are a matter of preference but the importance of the exercise combining responsible intention with business acumen cannot be overstated and group projects of this form are very valuable. Their importance merits a significant amount of assessment and works well to complement the other forms covered above.

However one arranges evaluation, the primary consideration is that it be used to *further learning*. The group assignment and the short tests (contributing in the range of 20% each to final grades) are quite straightforward and accord with much of the standardized mode of contemporary education, but they are a lesser part of the process. It is the reflective writings (worth 60% or more) that really open the way for more expansive and personal demonstrations of student learning. Young people generally *love* being assessed through reflective writings as it allows them to demonstrate their intelligence in far more holistic ways. Many find these challenges inspiring in their ability to generate self-revelation and a host of realizations about the contemporary world and their place in it.

Resourcing and Lecturing in Educating
for Responsibility

As mentioned previously, the resources teachers use need not be limited to the confines of the formal disciplinary literature. In pulling together materials to support and expand learning many other sources and media can be used to complement mainstream academic thinking. The main requirement is that all resources be relevant, accurate, engaging, informative, and thought-provoking.

In pulling together readings I search far and wide for writing that is well-researched, eye-opening and as much as possible, fascinating and inspiring. The final element in particular is important for illustrating the potential an expanded sense of responsibility has for making the world a better place. I have mentioned before the general aridity of this disciplinary literature but it is particularly its tendency to sacrifice breadth of perspective for depth of analysis that limits its potential as a sufficient worldview. To understand the interwoven complexity that surrounds us, learners cannot be restricted to just one discipline in the search for adequate context. Writings that transcend disciplinary boundaries open up tremendous possibilities to make connected learning maximally relevant to the present. There are profound, perspective-shifting insights to be found in autobiography, investigative journalism, magazines, historical documents, and fiction all of which can extend and link learning across domains. Students greatly appreciate the opportunity to become literally "more widely read" and making connections across subject areas is hugely empowering and indeed enlightening for a great number.

If the reader looks at a sample readings package in Appendix III, one can see that these additional resources can be very diverse indeed—and these are only the written resources. In a typical 12-week course in educating *for* responsibility, numerous visual resources are provided each week to contextualize advancing discussions and connect new ideas and insights. The internet is awash in streaming documentaries, video archives, and shared social media that provide a rich source of perspective when connecting an emerging sense of responsibility to the trends and happenings of the larger world. Everything one needs to build insightful perspective can be found in documentaries on the debt crisis in Europe, climate change, the history of money, life in the world's megacities, the impacts of the water crisis, the meaning of homelessness, the history of oil, the future of food, and the contemporary transformation of China among other themes. Many global news sites keep excellent archives that are very useful in making connections in students' minds and in a visual form that they are increasingly familiar with.

Learners can be linked not only to readings and videos but also to websites that are particularly authoritative on critical themes. Links will be posted to the journals Nature and Science for example as these are major outlets for some of the best and most readable science on climate disruptions and ecosystem dynamics (along with many other things of interest). Links can also be made to many reports on the state of the world and to the major news stories that emerge during a period of teaching in order that we can tie what we are learning to them. And of course, a central body of more academic information should also be provided, some in readings, but more in mini periods of lecturing to cover particularly foundational perspectives.

I save a lot of the more academic perspective for lecturing because I find that if the important themes can be conveyed in a simple way, it saves the whole inefficient dynamic of having students reluctantly wade through dense prose to get to the point. I keep up with the literature and as any need for more formal evidence or argument arises, I can interject and integrate as necessary. Mini lectures are critical supports in the whole structuring of learning and as each core theme is explored, a targeted package of resources provides support for further learning. In working to expand responsible potential, these resources play three key roles.

First, they broaden the mind. Asking learners to stretch their boundaries of understanding outwards to include what is happening in the slums of Brazil, or the forests of Indonesia, or how empathy works, or money markets, or how other cultures view responsibility, is excellent practice for expanding horizons and building more inclusive worldviews. Underlying educating *for* responsibility is a model that sees limitation as existing in time, in the extensive present and in depth. Thought of in this way, readings can be given that stretch thinking in all of these dimensions simultaneously. Rather than giving a selection of resources that relate to a single narrow theme or support a unidimensional viewpoint, I often use multidimensional resources that appear widely disconnected from each other in order to challenge students to make connections and see across boundaries. Such integrative connections can only be found by thinking deeply in terms of fundamental principles and broadly to include the width of debate and topic. Eclectic resources given in a variety of forms are excellent fodder for the expanding mind to contemplate as they directly challenge short-sightedness, narrow-mindedness, and superficiality.

A second role that resources play is to familiarize learners with the central literature of the discipline. In areas of ethics and responsibility, the foundational understandings of major schools of thought such as CSR, utilitarianism, Kantian thinking, virtue ethics and so on should be covered. We would do well to broaden these considerably though and include other global viewpoints such as Buddhism, Hinduism, Islam, indigenous perspectives, evolutionary thought, and positive psychology as equally relevant sources of perspective. In all cases though, the use of such materials should be two-fold—first, to build integration across a variety of interconnecting domains, and second to consolidate the conclusions that learners have themselves been challenged to arrive at. One of the most egregiously suboptimal aspects of the dominant model is to present theories, utilitarianism for example, as dead inheritances from some past historical age. Presented as abstract, authoritative answers to the complex question of what it is to be responsible, they are typically grossly oversimplified and purified for easy passive digestion. It is far from optimal practice and a fairly vain effort given the organic ways learners will really make their decisions in the future. It is much better to introduce utilitarianism to *validate* students' own conclusions on the need to think inclusively about the greatest good for the greatest number. Because they spontaneously apply this "law" to building visions of a better world (one that is more equal, more inclusive, more respectful etc.), learners don't need to be taught it in a tabula rasa fashion. But validating these inherent wisdoms, and giving them formal encouragement by showing that many sage minds have also reached this same conclusion, is very effective practice. It makes learning for responsibility much more resilient through the confidence gained by such expert validation. It makes the formal theories, and the cultural views they represent much more meaningful too as these come to be validated by personal perspective.

The extent to which any theory represents a universal truth is the extent to which the processes they point to can be found in all of us. If a utilitarian calculus of cost and benefit is a truly human tool then we should be able to see it operating within ourselves quite easily. Even in the first core theme above, learners employ Kantian imperatives, Buddhist compassion, Christian love, and a utilitarian calculus as they articulate visions for a better world. Reading formal theory follows as a confirmation of the value of these ways of personal thinking and this is hugely effective in bolstering feelings of accomplishment and conferring the sense of ethical acuity necessary for confidently exercising more responsible action.

A third underestimated benefit of excellent resources is their ability to extend learning beyond the limits of the classroom walls. When learners are particularly struck by articles, or book chapters or visual footage in particular, they share these among their peers and this often extends far outwards through social media like Facebook. I find that key clips, websites and documentaries are often uploaded and spread widely and I know also that these are regularly the topic of in-depth dinner table conversations. In their writings students regularly refer to long heated discussions with friends, family, and flatmates as they share resources, ask for advice, and pass on challenges. Educating should not be limited by the boundaries of the classroom and if there are opportunities to both send perspective-building out into broader society, and also have a broader sense come into the classroom (as when others' opinions are sought for assignments), it creates a cross-fertilization, a reality-check, and a strong test of relevance. Carefully picked resources that genuinely grab and hold intelligent attention are extremely valuable in helping this happen.

The Deeper Challenges of Educating *for* Responsibility

Taken together, the elements covered to this point will hopefully provide some glimpse of what educating *for* responsibility entails The reasons, prerequisites, ways and results of engaging it have all been discussed, albeit briefly. I could endlessly drill into the details of practice but that would distract from the broader brushstrokes used to this point. My aim here is not to provide an exhaustive users' manual, but a context for thinking differently about teaching for responsibility. Before ending though, there are two other themes that merit brief attention if the approach described here is to be seen in adequate context. The first is the challenge that educating *for* responsibility provides for the teacher. The second is the challenge it produces for business schools and the business world in general.

Challenges for the Teacher

To work in the open and collaborative way explained in this work is to step beyond the safety of education as usual where so much is organized to make teaching life unchallenging. When learners study only the narrow range of ideas the teacher is already familiar with, little unexpected learning occurs. When conversations are limited only to the central discipline, little big-picture learning emerges. And when students are rendered passive and anxious, little of value happens at all. If we were to be brutally honest, much of education as usual is dull and inconsequential for students no matter how we try to liven things up. The mode of engagement that educating *for* responsibility brings to the fore is entirely different for student and teacher alike.

For the teacher, moving into more open, liberated spaces where emotion, doubt, and difference are encouraged demands a different form of engagement—one which requires a wholly human presence in the classroom. As talking *at* students becomes talking *with* students, all sorts of unexpected material enters the classroom and it takes spontaneous creativity to juggle the range of conversations into meaningful perspectives that can further learning. This however, is one of the great attractions of teaching in more open ways. Rather than the dull safety of knowing that nothing unexpected is going to disrupt a carefully planned monologue, open process work means entering the classroom never knowing exactly what is going to emerge as we proceed through our deliberations. Working with a basic respect for student input, all emergent ideas need to be dealt with in ways that maintain momentum and preclude fruitless tangent. Teaching then comes to involve attention, sensitivity, spontaneity, and creativity in every meeting—qualities that make work highly stimulating and rewarding. It is much, much more enjoyable than the standard mode of unidirectional teaching.

The essential principle of *expanding* students' capacity for responsible thought and action means that the teacher needs to be expansive in their own perspective. To know where good resources lie, teachers need to be well read and increasingly "well watched." I bring history, future studies, politics, biology, philosophy, media, psychology, sociology, and religious studies to bear on the theme of responsibility and to do this I have to be familiar with these basic areas of study. Teachers should keep up with local and world news in order to make connections and keep discussions as contemporary and relevant as possible. It is also good to post documentaries which are a particularly useful media. Visual footage manages to convey an emotional connection that prose rarely does and in extending boundaries of care, films and documentaries are inordinately effective.

In the end, educating *for* responsibility encourages students to expand beyond the limits of short-sightedness, narrow-mindedness, and superficiality in their dealings with the world. This requires that the teacher challenge their own limitations if they are to deal with the core questions that will emerge in open discussion. They will need to be non-defensive and able to deal with a range of queries ranging from the history of capitalism to the rise of China, the nature of the sovereign debt crisis, the psychology of compassion, the politics of global trade, the ecology of the oceans, and a host of other considerations. The constant challenge to integrate and understand the contemporary world will veer into these and a hundred other themes. The more widely informed the teacher is, the more they will be prepared for the challenge.

Responsibility is a pervasive concept and it naturally impinges on all the subject areas mentioned above as a matter of course, meaning that relevant materials can be found almost anywhere. This makes the background work for teaching far more enjoyable as the search for resources goes far into the unknown, broadening and deepening the teacher's perspective in useful and enlightening ways. To work well, the teacher has to be deeply interested in furthering their own perspective, learning new things, taking on board new considerations, and building more accomplished understandings on what it is to be responsible. This is what we demand of our students and educating *for* responsibility works best when both learner and teacher collaborate in the search for better worldviews.

Although these challenges may seem onerous they are not in fact and the positive atmosphere created by treating young people respectfully pays huge dividends. Teaching in collaborative ways is informative, exciting, refreshing, challenging, fulfilling, and fun for all involved. As a teacher it calls upon a range of broad capabilities that amount to being more human in the classroom and as such, it is a richly rewarding way to work.

Challenges for Business Schools

Perhaps the greatest challenge inherent in educating *for* responsibility is the one posed by the pressure to conform to mainstream practice. It will be clear by now that in application this more emergent approach involves overturning many of the fundamental assumptions of education as usual and as such will be seen by many as being highly radical—as indeed it is. The important thing though is that the learning is highly valued by students and this is the evidence that I have found to be most compelling to the in-place powers that be. Opening a space for this type of learning in many business schools will require that the innovator constantly defend and justify deviations from standard practice. Smaller classes, open process, and collaboration may need much explanation but this need not be an awkward process as long as there is a genuine commitment to learning at the apex of the institution. Any teacher experimenting with change will be constantly asked to explain what they are doing and why it might work well. Among other things, this gives the institution a chance to learn and grow too as it allows the innovation and the creativity so often recommended for others to be practiced in its own classrooms.

In reality though, many business schools are strongly wedded to education as usual for a host of reasons that would merit a book in themselves to explain. Suffice it to say that there is always likely to be resistance to change in any bureaucratic institution and that significant time might be required to secure the prerequisite conditions for an in-depth education *for* responsibility. But the cause is a worthy one and business schools *ought* to be challenged to do more than many do in bolting a half-hearted education *about* responsibility onto unchanged degree programs in the hope that this will change the world for the better. As educators specifically challenged with empowering young people to improve the world, we have a professional responsibility to challenge established practices wherever they undermine this end.

Given the state of the world it is clear that whatever is being done in the name of encouraging business to be more responsible is having an insufficient impact. As the real world really slips toward chaotic and dreadful outcomes, driven in no small part by business as usual, this and the education as usual that supports it, have to change. Any teachers mindful of this and keen to try new techniques may uncover deeper sources of resistance than simply clinging to teaching habits. Business schools are usually very much aligned to the priorities of business as usual and see market freedom and economic growth as necessary goods of supreme importance. Some simply ignore the larger trends happening beyond the narrow confines of market faithfulness and the challenge implicit in educating differently can bring heated responses—as challenges to all fundamentalist faiths tend to do. However, the reality is that educating *for* responsible business practice is not anti-business but wholly pro-business on the condition that it advances the thriving of the whole. Currently, the biggest threat to business *is* business as usual, and contrary to what some may feel about the "soft" areas of ethics and social responsibility, it is only by developing these qualities that business will be able to thrive into the future. Without their cultivation, the current harvest of unrestrained growth and irresponsible business—unmanageable debt, global polarization, depleting resources—will bring an inevitable economic implosion.

In a more farsighted, broad-minded, and deeply considered perspective, we should have by now moved far beyond the old nostrum that "the business of business is business." In the contemporary world business has been granted such power that it now impacts ecological, climactic and social boundaries in seriously dangerous ways. As such, the real business of business includes considering all of these domains as its actions increasingly dictate their thriving or depletion. We have moved beyond the era when business can see its responsibilities as existing only to itself. Those in teaching positions that continue to shape an oblivious faith in young people that business as usual *can* continue into the future are not preparing them well for their futures as business people, or as citizens for that matter.

This generation of young people is entering into a rapidly changing world, one characterized by declining indices of fertility, biodiversity, food, and water security, climate stability, and social harmony. They, more than any generation of business students, will be called upon to engage an extraordinary responsibility if they are to correct these declines. Yet, as things stand we seem to be insufficiently creative and rather too complacent in exercising our own responsibility to find optimal ways of helping them develop their inherent capacities for considerate, farsighted, and wise being in the world.

What I have shared here is certainly not *the* best way to teach *for* responsibility but it is certainly much more effective than the standard model. Having begun with that and moved my way to this, I know just how effective the shift can be and hopefully a little of that has been conveyed in these pages. The most important qualities for acting responsibly include a broad and extensive understanding that sees the connections between personal action and collective outcomes. It also involves a commitment to ensure that the future is at least as good as the present. It requires the ability to exercise self-restraint and see through the rationalizations self-indulgence spins. Responsibility requires the ability to defend and articulate deeply considered values and to listen to and find common ground with others pushing for positive change. In educating *for* responsibility all of these capacities are exercised and it is this that sets the approach apart from merely educating *about* responsibility.

For any teacher cognizant of the trials of our times and keen to assist young people prepare to overcome them, this general framework might offer some immediately practical options. It is challenging, but ultimately rewarding for students, teachers, and institutions alike as all learning processes should be. Education as usual cannot solve the problems of business as usual as it is part and parcel of its continuance. In these increasingly unusual times we need more effective approaches to be tried and shared. What I have called educating *for* responsibility in these pages is one tested method that has far-reaching results. I hope that it stimulates others to experiment with it in whatever form they like as it really can help young people see their responsibilities for the future in a far clearer light.

Applying Educating *for* Responsibility in Other Contexts

Although the preceding discussion has applied itself specifically to structured undergraduate programs, the approach can be easily adapted to fit other contexts. The adaptability of educating *for* responsibility comes from the fact that the critical contents (what a better world looks like, what values are required, the barriers to constructive engagement, and the ways we can work to build a better world) are constructed by the learners themselves. This allows a generic process to cross cultural boundaries with ease and this process has been used successfully in a range of different cultural contexts as the imperatives of knowing where we want to go, the things that stand in our way, and the ways in which we can overcome these are of equal significance to all. Educating *for* responsibility has accordingly been used in various combinations with groups from Samoa to Bhutan.

Flexibility is also served by the ease with which component parts of the process can be de-coupled from the whole and used alone or in novel combination. Thus, in a business context, intensive workshops can be designed to clarify collective ideals and values, and to discern direct ways in which any business can better serve explicitly positive outcomes. The collaboration involved releases collective wisdom and a breadth of perspective in focused and manageable ways—allowing teams at all organizational levels to more acutely perceive where, when, and how opportunities for greater responsibility can be created. Educating *for* responsibility is an empowering process intended to release the potential to think more inclusively and deeply about our obligations in an inter-connected world and as such it can add usefully to a range of future planning or scenario work. An increasing number of forward-thinking organizations are coming to realize that business as usual will be increasingly untenable in the decades ahead and are, through a variety of means, actively engaging foresight as they plan for navigating uncertain times. Although these techniques allow for a more considered view of what will be required for future thriving, the focus still tends to be overly narrow as the organization's wellbeing is commonly assumed to be the main, if not the only outcome of interest. In an increasingly interconnected world this thinking is too conflict-inducing to be useful so the basic structure of educating *for* responsibility aims at a broader and deeper analysis of where truly constructive interventions can be made to improve the whole upon which the organization depends. The future will demand a far greater harmonizing of business with the other constituencies that allow it to thrive and economic strategy needs to be developed in a more farsighted, broadly conceived and deeply considered modality. This is the mode encouraged by the approach described here and could be creatively used by business to the benefit of many constituencies both now and in the future.

This basic focus on liberating a responsible potential can also be very useful to organizations in opening up opportunities for individuals to identify where and how they can work to better harmonize the outcomes experienced by self, business, society, and planet. Many younger professionals have a strong commitment to working in sustainable and inclusive ways and organizations that encourage creative thinking around how such positive values can be embraced become far more attractive options for many. Educating *for* responsibility can create a useful and highly efficient template for intensive workshops seeking to align organizational imperatives with those of the larger community or the local environment and the range is limited only by the creativity of those involved. At root though, whatever strategic application forward-thinking organizations wish to put it to, this approach works in large part due to the respect it gives to participants' views, ideas, and feelings. Educating *for* responsibility empowers people to grow into a more broad-minded, farsighted, and deeply considered awareness and to use this to discern better ways of working. It is then a powerful tool for focusing and forging a commitment to responsible change and where this is genuinely desired by an organization, the various techniques and exercises outlined here hold considerable promise in achieving this important end.

In this sense, the approach can also find a useful place in working with any group needing more precision in their vision of what a better world is and how they might work for its emergence. School-age participants are particularly receptive to its sensible basic structure, although care should be taken with the components asking for personal accountability as these need to be tempered when used with younger groups. In other educational contexts, the basic template is broadly applicable and if the final theme, where responsible intention is combined with professional skill (in the above, by designing responsible businesses) is used, its utility expands. Thus, engineering students or student teachers can be asked to explore the practical ways in which they can work as responsible engineers or educators to help ensure a better world. Those studying to enter into any professional career can usefully be asked to consider their chosen profession and see in detail how it could work for others co-benefit. How can they best use their qualifications to promote a more responsible order? This is a fundamentally important question for all young people to ask themselves in these times.

Although the structuring of deliberations in all such applications is critical in directing attention and effort, it is above all the spirit of the engagement that is ultimately important. Educating *for* responsibility is grounded in treating participants, whoever they may be, as complex and intelligent people with the potential and the human desire to secure a more harmonious world for all. The approach described is designed to create a humanizing space within which this potential can be cultivated and honed. As the need to expand such spaces becomes more pressing, educating *for* responsibility can find an increasing applicability across many sectors.

APPENDIX I

Sample Assignment Outlines

These are only a few of the many reflective writings that students are asked to write on. They vary a good deal in specific wording from semester to semester but I have included here an assignment outline for each of the five core themes covered during the course of learning for responsibility. Assessed writings on personal inconsistency and enacting greater responsibility (core questions 3 and 4) are always included as assessed work given the importance of bringing focused attention to these practical exercises. The others are more variable and may be given in a variety of forms and lengths.

In these examples, a few practical considerations should become clear including the importance of detailed instructions on writing and making the purpose of assessment as clear as possible. Note also that writing assignment outlines gives the opportunity to explicitly build on the unfolding understandings learners have already come to.

Example 1(a): What Does a Better World Look Like?

Assignment

As you will know from reading the course outline, each of these collective exercises contributes 10% toward your final grade. Each writing assignment will connect to and build upon the discussions we are having in class.

In the last few sessions we have been developing a framework that will allow us to anchor our evaluative judgments according to shared and robust criteria as to what "better" and "worse" worlds look like for this group. The criteria we have developed have been worked out in small and large group discussions and this first writing exercise involves a final testing of these through talking to others around you and personally reflecting on the utility of the criteria articulated to date.

The question asked of you in class was as follows:

Do you think that the dimensions developed by the class represent a common set of essential human aspirations? Why/Why not?

Now a few words of explanation are in order before tackling the issue of writing per se.

First of all, please note that the dimensions referred to can be found on the course page under the "resources" tab. You will also find here the original lists developed by the two groups (one believing that the world will be better in 2020, the other believing that it will be worse in 2020). Some of these specifics disappeared in the large group deliberations and you might want to refer back to the original lists to see if anything essential has disappeared that you think needs to be included.

Second in this question, the word aspiration is used and this refers to the "better" end of the various dimensions developed by the class. Answering the question then involves considering these positive criteria and judging whether in your mind, these do indeed capture common human aspirations.

Notes on Writing

- I realize that for some of you the general encouragement to think deeply about the question will seem rather loose. In most classes you are given much more specific guidelines that tell you explicitly what to include and what not to include. My feeling is that in this class where the emphasis is on developing your own rigorous and defensible worldview, such detailed structuring works against free and open expression. The criteria for grading are that you demonstrate genuine thoughtfulness and show a genuine engagement with the question.
- The question asks you to make your own judgment as to whether these dimensions represent common human aspirations or not. I have been asked if library research is necessary and the answer to

this is no. I am not interested in the opinions of others but in your own opinion. Heading off into the literature will have little to contribute and is likely to lead to a substituting of others' thinking for your own voice. If you want to do a quick survey of broader opinion as to the nature of human aspiration you are free to do so, but whatever conclusions others might have formed should be used only as input into your own judgment and should not be a substitute for it.

- A more feasible and enjoyable means of exploring the legitimacy of the dimensions you developed is to talk with other people around you. What do your friends or family think of these dimensions? Do they ring true for them or do they think that other criteria capture our common aspirations more meaningfully? If they have alternative views, reflect upon them and if they stand up to your own personal scrutiny, adjust or amend the working list of dimensions to reflect this new understanding.

- Given that your writing is about your own thoughts on the matter it should be in the first person and you should clearly own the conclusions you derive as your own. Thus, writing in the form of "I believe…," "I think…," etc., is the most appropriate mode.

- The guiding word limit has been set at 1,000 words but this is an approximation. If you find you have more to say and that 1,000 words are not sufficient to capture the breadth of your thinking on this question, you can keep writing. I see no good pedagogical reason to stop you developing your ideas to fit an arbitrary word count. Having said that though, I do expect that if you go beyond the suggested length that additional arguments are made in a succinct manner and that you don't engage in repetition. From previous experience I can say (for those concerned that their own efforts might pale in comparison to the more bulky offerings of others) that few go far beyond the recommended length.

- In saying that your writing will be graded on the depth of thinking it reveals I want to encourage you to do just that—think about it. The more you talk with others and find quiet space to reflect upon it, the better your answer is likely to be.

- The writing is due in class on Monday and given that there are around 6 hours of out-of-class time allocated for this course, I expect everyone to have it in by then. Given that this is part of a sequential and collaborative process there will be little to no flexibility around submitting this late. In other words, get it in or you get 0%.

• If you have any questions please don't hesitate to get in touch by e-mail. Please note though that I will not read draft answers as this typically constitutes a double-grading which is of dubious fairness to others.

Thank you.

Example 1(b): Imagining Better and Worse Worlds

(This more creative writing was designed to help a class more fully imagine what the differences between an improving and declining world might be by writing letters back to themselves from imagined futures that portray the realities of what life would be like in a "better" or "worse" world.)

Writing

The aim of this first reflective writing is to consolidate our views of what the future might entail by exploring the most optimistic and pessimistic possibilities for how life in New Zealand might be in the year 2020. To do this you are asked to do the following:

1. Write one page (standard 10pt font) that paints as engaging a picture as you can of what conditions will be like if things turn out for the worst in the year 2020. This should be in the form of a letter to yourself from the future that gives as clear and compelling a sense of how life will be at that point if things deteriorate towards the "worse" end of the continuum (that we have been anchoring in conditions of increased conflict and competition with others). How would it look? How would it feel? How would the environment, global society and local life be faring? Would it be pleasant, safe, happy? Thinking along these lines should help bring the picture of possible decline to life.

2. Write one page that paints as engaging a picture as you can of what conditions will be like if things turn out for the best in the year 2020.

This should take the same form of a letter to yourself from the future that gives a clear and engaging sense of how life would be if things improved towards the "better" end of the continuum—anchored in conditions of increased harmony and cooperation with others. How would it look? How would it feel? How would the environment, global society and local life be faring?

3. Draw a continuum that ranges from "worse" to "better" in accordance with the general model of the possible future that we have been exploring in class with the "worse" end being on the left and the "better" end being on the right. *This continuum should consist of a line that is 10cm long* (this will be important in bringing feedback on the collective responses back to the class as a whole). Place on this continuum three marks that correspond to (a) where you think we were in 2000, (b) where you think things will be in 2020, and (c) where you *want* things to be in 2020. Clearly label these points on the continuum.

4. Finally, write one page answering the following question as thoughtfully as you can.

How important will creating a shift towards a greater concern for others be in reaching the point you want us to reach in 2020? (i.e. in reaching point (c) above).

The point of this question is to explore the centrality (or otherwise) of ethical improvement in producing a positive future.

Notes

- It is important to keep your scenarios in the realm of possibility. So while it is very helpful to fully explore the realms of what might happen, stop short of painting scenarios that you think are wholly unrealistic.
- The suggested length of each piece is a guideline only. Doing less than a page for each part would not be acceptable but if you find that writing more is helpful to you then by all means continue writing.
- Please make your writing in the first person. I realize that this goes against much of your formal training in this environment but it is

important to write personally as the aim here is to elucidate your own values, thoughts and feelings.
- The criteria for this assessment are as discussed in class and center upon your level of genuine application. Thus, evidence of having thought about these issues seriously and deeply will serve you well.
- It will help considerably if you find the chance to talk about these issues with your friends, family and/or classmates.

Thanks

Example 2: Personal Evaluations of Responsibility

Values and the Self

In class we have been developing an evaluative framework that allows us to clearly discern what is progressive and what is regressive in terms of collective and individual action. The class as a whole expressed a strong desire to live in a world that is ecologically healthy, socially inclusive, and free from the depredations of conflict and violence. I think that most people would wholeheartedly agree that this would constitute a desirable state of affairs.

In light of this, we have been exploring what values, or characteristics, or potentials need to be nurtured and spread if this desirable future is to be secured. I will give you a detailed breakdown of this when we meet next week but the criteria you developed in small groups emphasized the following the most:

Compassion (mentioned 24 times)
Honesty (mentioned 16 times)
Generosity (mentioned 10 times)
Respect (mentioned 9 times)

This is a useful set of core characteristics and no doubt the world would be much improved if these were more to the fore. However, when we think of these things in the abstract as we have been doing, it is all too easy to see these as necessary qualities for other people to live by and to leave ourselves conveniently out of the picture. Given that you raised these qualities as critical ones, I want you to now put yourselves firmly within this framework of analysis.

Exercise

1. For this writing I want you to discuss your own development on each one of these dimensions in turn. To do this, please create a scale for each dimension that ranges from 1–7 and which is anchored on the right hand side by the positive characteristic mentioned above (compassionate, honest, generous, respectful) and on the left by their opposites. For present purposes, if you label these as uncaring, dishonest, greedy, and disrespectful that would help us form some orderly conclusions. So how do you rate on each one of these four critical dimensions?
I am not interested in how you want to be in the future or how you think you have been in the past, but about how you think you are right now. Be honest as there is nothing to gain by being less than this—and of course it is something that you say you value highly.

2. Once you have rated yourself, I want you to identify the single action that best exemplifies putting each of these positive values to work in your own life *over the past two weeks*. When in the last fortnight did you act with real compassion and when did you act with particular honesty, generosity, and respect? You should briefly recount one action for each characteristic and choose what you think best exemplifies this virtue. Be concise and don't write more than a few sentences for each. Please note that the information that you give is disclosure that you should be comfortable with. Nothing will be shared with others in the class for obvious reasons but in the few instances where some might feel awkward mentioning specifics, edit the content or examples accordingly.

3. Having done this for each positive characteristic, I would like you to think carefully about your self-evaluations. When you think about where you currently stand, why is your score not more accomplished? What is it that prevents you from acting more compassionately, honestly, generously, and respectfully? This is a question that requires genuine reflection and most of the evaluation will be based on your really grappling with it. Given that we see these qualities as being

critical, and given that we will be less than perfect in our development, what is it that is holding us back really? I think it is the most important question that we could ask ourselves at this point.

4. Finally, I need you all to pick two people who know you well. Ask each of these people (who ought to be long-standing friends, family members or flatmates) to rate you on the same set of four scales. How compassionate, honest, generous, and respectful do they think you are? The point of this is to get a reality check and for you to self-assess with these others opinions somewhere in mind. Now, there are a couple of extremely important points relating to this process.

First of all, it is absolutely essential that these assessments be kept private. The two people who will assess you should be given an envelope to put their evaluations in, or should be asked to staple the paper or secure it in whatever way will ensure privacy. *On no account are you allowed to look at these, highly tempting though that might be.* You cannot ask them how they rated you as that is between them and me. Remember that honesty and respect are core aspects of character and you have to live up to these for this exercise.

Notes

a. You need to provide all four components of this exercise on the due date.
b. The length should be up to four pages given the complexity involved. Approximately half of the writing should deal with part (3) above—what is it that is holding you back?
c. You are not being judged in any way on your self-rankings but only on your honest and deeply thoughtful engagement with this question.

We can address any issues relating to this in class on Monday.

Thank you.

Example 3: Accounting for Discrepancy

As explained in class, this writing is designed to build on the understandings raised in the previous writing. The purpose here then is to explore further the tensions between our own self-interest and the interests of broader constituencies.

At the start of this class, you identified a series of outcomes that you deem to be desirable states of being for our shared future. Central to this vision was a desire to bring forth a more sustainable and equal (or inclusive) state of being. In this writing I would like you to consider your own consumption habits in relation to these ideals.

Writing

1. Taking the criteria of a more sustainable and a more inclusive/equal world I would like you to identify the things that you purchase at least once a week that compromise your ability to be seen as a genuine force for improvement on these two dimensions. In other words, when you look at your regular purchases, what stands out as being most harmful to the goal of contributing to a more sustainable and inclusive/equal world?

2. Once you have identified two questionable items that you regularly purchase (one working against sustainability and one against inclusiveness/equality) I would like you to outline the excuses that you find yourself making to justify your continued use of these two items in light of your understanding that they may be far from helpful in building a better world. In other words, how do you explain the discrepancy between your ideals of a more sustainable and inclusive world and your actual behavior as a consumer? Comment on how valid you think these excuses actually are.

Notes

As with previous writings this is to be a reflective piece and the depth and authenticity of your writing that is key. This is not something where you should try to discern the politically correct answer as we are aiming to understand the common dynamics that operate within us all through this exercise.

Please note that you need to talk about two regular purchases (one that is unsustainable and one that is polarizing) and that we agreed not to include petrol as one of the items you can discuss as the problems with this are quite familiar to most. It is not an exercise in beating yourself up with guilt, but rather an open-eyed attempt to place ourselves within the idealistic context developed in the abstract.

Length guidelines are the same as last time and if you have any questions, send me an e-mail.

Thank you

Example 4: Acting Generously

(This example asks learners to go beyond their normal limitations to act with greater virtue. Among other things, the potential to use assignment outlines to integrate previous learning is made evident here.)

Introduction

In recent classes we have been discussing some of the limitations of Western rational approaches to ethics and how these can become more truly rationalizing than rational in practice. Utilitarian calculation for example, are prone to self-serving biases whereby the relative costs and benefits are calculated to accord with self-interested outcomes, so defeating the purpose of the dispassionate analysis that these ideally employ. This applies even to the "corrections" that theorists like John Rawls would encourage us to adopt in order to avoid such consequences (see readings online). There are other approaches that argue that a more effective means of reaching critical ethical outcomes involves realization rather than rationalization and accordingly, major themes in virtue ethics and a variety of other cultural approaches (such as Hinduism or Buddhism) would encourage individuals to enact good conduct and through this, come to an understanding of the value of genuine considerateness. In a sense such approaches believe in changing behavior first and allowing the rational understanding to follow rather than the other way around. For this writing I would like you to practically explore the validity of such an approach in action.

Assignment

Over the next two weeks, take two days when your time is not dominated by external demands. During these days I would like you to try to cultivate a genuine attitude of helpfulness towards others and to see the day as a series of opportunities to contribute to others' wellbeing and happiness. This will involve a subtle but deep shift in attitude, a central component of which will involve reducing the focus on your own immediate outcomes as you become more focused on the possibilities each day presents to be kind, considerate and generous towards others. To do this you need to have openness not only of attitude, but of time to employ this shift freely.

What I would like you to do is enter into the days you choose with a conscious attitude that sees the day as an opportunity to contribute. This is not meant to mean grand gestures, but rather manageable acts of civility and kindness. You should not engage with any actions that you are really uncomfortable with nor engage in any actions that are likely to be genuinely against your interests (such as giving money you really can't afford, or putting yourself in situations that might risk significantly negative outcomes for yourself). However, having said that, to make this work you will need to push yourself beyond your normal limits and be more helpful and considerate than you would normally be. Thus, you should be stepping beyond your normal habitual behaviors but judiciously so.

It is up to you to decide how far you want to take this exercise but at no point should you feel like you are a martyr to an unreasonable cause. Whatever you do should be done with goodwill and not with resentment. I will refrain from giving concrete suggestions as this would work against the attentiveness to your own life that this aims to explore. There are a myriad of opportunities for contributing to others' lives that present themselves on a daily basis if we are open to them.

Writing

For the writing I want you to report openly and honestly on how you find the experience and to include in your write-up the following—along with whatever else you have learned or observed during this exercise.

1. Two specific incidents that you can describe in some detail of how an act of kindness or helpfulness was experienced by yourself and the other(s) that were involved directly in the dynamic. For each incident, describe what happened and its context in brief terms. Explain

how you felt before, during, and after performing the act of kindness. Describe how the other person(s) reacted and reflect upon what this interaction did in terms of the immediate relationships (if this is applicable) between you and the others involved—were they improved qualitatively or not?

2. Directly address issues of how challenging it was to act in this actively considerate state of mind. Was it difficult or easy? Why? What barriers or negative feelings did you find yourself experiencing as you thought of acting kindly and while you were in the process of acting in this mode?

3. Talk about whether, overall, you found this to be a positive experience in terms of making you feel better about yourself and others around you. Did you feel more proud of yourself at the end of these interactions or not? Did they make you feel more positive about the world around you and your place in it?

4. Discuss whether such a process of "pushing oneself" to be more generous would be a valuable practice to engage in more regularly in your daily life.

Notes

- The writing for this assignment is more qualitative and less structured than most. As a result you are free to go beyond the specifics outlined above to include other dimensions that you think are important to discuss.

- The balance of writing is up to you but I am imagining at this point that part 1 above will occupy about a third of the writing but you can vary the proportion as long as all of the questions are covered adequately.

- The assessment criteria are the genuineness of your engagement with the question, the attentiveness to detail that you bring to conducting the actions, and the depth and breadth of the reflection you apply to the experience.

A final note is in order and that concerns length. In class there were both expressions of support for word limits and others against such limits.

I want to keep the length open and not to constrain reflection and deep analysis by the imposition of an across-the-board word limit. I maintain a position that sees exploration as important and sees little reason to prevent anyone who is genuinely stimulated into more in-depth discussion from doing so. This would to me at least, go against the whole spirit and purpose of education and compromise its potential. Having said this though, I do expect answers to be targeted to the question and any longer writings need to be focused and to the point. I think that some may harbor feelings that longer writings by others will make their shorter ones be downgraded by comparison but this is not the case. The normal range of writing for this would be in the range of 2,000–3,000 words and those that go beyond this enter into a category that goes beyond the normal call of duty and if they do a good job they will be rewarded accordingly. For the vast majority who do not go as far, normal grading criteria apply and you will not be brought down by the exceptional performance of others.

This writing is due on the Monday of week 8 in class. If you have any questions let me know by e-mail or in class.

Thank you

Example 5: Designing Businesses for a Better World

(This is a sample outline that challenges students to put their business skills to use in the service of the values and the world they aspire to. In most instances this is a group assignment done over many weeks. Here the time was shorter and designed for personal reflection prior to having groups pick the best ideas and advance them together.)

Introduction

Having spent the majority of our time to date outlining the nature of a better world, what values need to be cultivated to achieve that, how these might be socially facilitated, and what prevents us from acting more responsibly, it is now time to move onto a new stage of our learning where we actively consider how we might contribute to creating that better world by developing responsible enterprises. This writing accordingly asks you to develop original ideas that could be put into practice in order to build a more sustainable, just, secure, and peaceful world.

The ethical goals which we agreed on early in our discussions fit well with the framework of the Earth Charter which is a well-known and highly respected blueprint for responsible and progressive social action. What you are asked to do for this writing is to think of a creative and practical business idea that would accord with the principles of the Earth Charter. This means that whatever ideas you develop cannot use resources unsustainably, cannot create significant volumes of waste, and cannot create social injustice. Ideally, your ideas should ultimately reduce these problems by helping to enhance sustainability, reduce waste and create greater levels of social justice. It is only through innovations of this kind, broadly conceived of as for-benefit (as opposed to for-profit per se) that we can begin to actively participate in creating the more peaceful, just and thriving world we want to see materialize.

To do this writing well you will have to:

1. Clearly show how your new innovation would help move us towards achieving a more just, sustainable, peaceful, and secure world.
2. Clearly show how there will be no significant social or environmental costs inherent in pursuing your idea.
3. Clearly show that your idea is practical and viable given current social, political, and economic realities.

Process

Remembering that this challenge involves you aligning your ideas with the spirit of the Earth Charter, a good place to start is reading the document itself which is posted online. You have also been directed to some websites including Worldchanging and Trendsetting as potential sources of online inspiration.

We will spend the next couple of meetings in group discussions to give you the chance to inspire one another's thinking and to test the practicality of your emerging ideas. In the meantime, as with all of these writings, the more you can talk with others around you, the better your ideas and writings are likely to be.

Thank you

Sample Feedback Documents

In the text above, the importance of giving good clear feedback was outlined. Here are two examples of collective feedback documents. The first was given in response to reflective writings on the subject of the positive values necessary for building a better world and what prevents us from engaging them more fully. The second example is feedback on writings about pushing action beyond normal boundaries.

In both cases it is useful to note the tone of feedback which is authoritative but not clumsily formal. Much encouragement is given along with the occasional bit of firmer feedback to the less engaged. The more important content though is the discussion of what the whole group was writing about and the major patterns in their thinking. Students greatly appreciate seeing how the whole group thought in its variety and in its commonality. Giving collective feedback in this form is enormously useful for bringing the essential themes to light which can then be integrated into discussion and built on.

In terms of assessment, as mentioned in the text, this is a qualitative and subtle process that cannot be concretely grasped without experimentation. Yet there should be enough here to allow those interested to grasp the essential dynamics.

Feedback on Reflective Writing #1

As I mentioned in class, I am taking a somewhat different approach to these assessments on the basis of trying to develop as rich a set of considerations as possible from the group as a whole. In answering this reflective writing you collectively covered a good deal of ground and brought out some very interesting considerations that are useful in helping us understand why we do not do more to enact our core values. In this document, I want to give a summary of some of the core considerations in order that we can build on these and advance our discussions.

General Comments on Performance

Overall, I was impressed by the thoughtfulness of your reflections which generally engaged with the questions set sincerely. There were a few papers which didn't push enquiry very far at all which is unfortunate in the sense that what you get out of these reflective writings is a direct function of what you put into them. I graded your writings according to the depth of thoughtfulness and the level of application revealed in your answers. Most did well, some could have done better, and some did not do too well. There are a host of specifics involved in assessing each grade but a generally useful way of understanding these is to consider how far they advance the class's understanding of values and the barriers to exercising these. You will find in the explanations below an account of where the deeper layers of the group's thinking lies and your own personal contributions to our collective understanding can be usefully assessed against the depth of these. There are some basic points that were raised by most, but some took the question much deeper to probe into the underlying reasons and dynamics and these are very useful in moving things forward. Those who explored these deeper ways of looking advance the class understanding the most and get the most credit. To the extent that you stopped short of a deeper reflection, your grade is less impressive.

Accounting for Your Own Actions

The first part of the question asked you to put yourself within the value framework that we have developed in the abstract and to assess your own conduct in terms of these metrics. You were asked to provide specific examples of behavior that demonstrated the virtues in action and to get two people you know to provide an evaluation of your standing on these values as they see you. This part of the writing was read to see that you had indeed done what was asked but the content was not assessed (for obvious reasons).

The range of behaviors was enormous and ranged from people speaking honestly to others about relationships, giving money and time (generally to friends and family) and what might be called random acts of kindness ranging from giving change to folks short of money at the checkout to a surprisingly large number of people who gave up seats on public transport. There were many instances of people really going out of their way to be involved in helping the community including quite a few dramatic examples of intervening to help kids, animals, and strangers in need. Read together, they give a very strong sense of how much good a group like this collectively does in the normal course of your lives. You may think that your own actions make no difference but combined with the similar actions of your peers, they most certainly do.

Before the break, we spoke about how your own self-evaluations related to the evaluations you made of "people in general" (early in the semester) and to the evaluations that your friends and family contributed. I don't want to recreate that discussion here. Suffice it to say that the first part of the question was done competently by all and I was genuinely impressed by your levels of engagement on these dimensions.

Explaining What Holds Us Back from Doing Better

This was the part of the reflection that was most important as explained in the set-up of the question. We know that the values you identified (generosity, compassion, respect, honesty, etc.) are essential for securing the collective outcomes we want to see in the future. Yet it is one thing to identify these and another thing entirely to try and live up to them in our lives. The question was really designed to have you explore within yourself, the reasons we hold ourselves back from engaging critical values more fully. It is an essential question for us to answer because if we can identify the things that really hold us back personally, then we are likely to understand the things that are holding us all back and how we might collectively address these.

In answering this question the class had an interesting variety of arguments which ranged from the relatively shallow to the profound. To make sense of these it is probably best to consider the values in sequence.

Respect

This value was the least problematic and the least discussed overall. Most wrote that in general they give respect to others, try to listen to opinions that are not their own, include people that are not part of their intimate group, and act with what was often referred to as "common courtesy." Many of you talked about respect as a close relative to tolerance, and reading between the lines, it was often this that engaged you most. Most people wrote of respect in an outward way—that you don't openly criticize or challenge people on points of difference, but that internally you are often in deep opposition. Such dynamics raise the question of how sincere this respect we speak of is, and how much it is an enacted mask that hides a deeper and more factual intolerance.

There was much discussion about people having to learn respect and I was quite surprised by how contingent the respect many of you give actually is. Lots of you described the conditions under which people would lose your respect and have no further claim upon any considerate action as a result. Some explored these ideas in depth to ask themselves why they were being so judgmental and to try and discern what the criteria for gaining and losing respect actually are in their own minds. Where people did this, the discussion delved deeper and revealed more interesting things. For those who stopped short at saying "others have to earn my respect" less was revealed.

Overall, respect was the least interesting of the categories that you wrote about and in general, the consensus was that respect is shown externally with great regularity but that respect is contingent upon the behavior of the person, or persons concerned.

Honesty

There were many more discussions about honesty than about respect and this took some intriguing forms. I noticed that a surprising number of you, when talking about the honest actions you had performed over the past fortnight, chose instead to point to where you had been dishonest. This occurred in about a third of the papers and was not the case for any other category (i.e. not many spent time talking about where they had failed to be generous or compassionate). I am unsure as to what this might signify but it was fairly striking.

In considering how you put this virtue into action, almost everybody mentioned that they employ "white lies" to ease social interaction and no doubt that is true of almost all of humanity. But the real question is, why do we do this? Most argued that lying, or not being entirely "straight up" is a strategy employed to benefit others. We don't want to be hurtful by telling others that they are out of line, not suited to us romantically, have a bad haircut, a terrible dress sense and so forth. Many mentioned in this context that there is a basic conflict between values in real life and that lying is sometimes necessary to further compassion. Such discussions were common in your writing.

The better papers took this theme a stage further by reflecting on how true this excuse of not hurting others actually is and found that in many instances, it is the other person *and* ourselves that we seek to protect by not being honest. Not only do we not want to hurt others but we fear the response that being honest might bring. You don't want to tell your partner that it is over because it will be painful and who knows what the reaction will be. So we put it off, go behind their back or (in a particularly male adaptation) act in ways that we hope can be read by another without us having to spell it out.

Those who broached the deeper layers of dishonesty generally mentioned how lying helps preserve the illusions that we want others to believe about ourselves. Thus, your mother asks how you did on an assignment and you tell her that you got a better grade. You exaggerate your involvement in a good cause, bend the truth about why you can't come to dinner and so on. A number of you explored the roots of this tendency and generally concluded that a fear of rejection by others is what most forcefully restricts your tendency to always be honest.

The best writings took the debate further to engage the critical issue of being honest with oneself. In general, honesty was only talked about in relation to others but in reality, we are often quite dishonest with ourselves and how we are in the world. We deny certain aspects of our conduct and being, we project problems onto others, we exaggerate our virtue. For those who did raise these issues it was a very thoughtful approach and the writings were accordingly of considerable value.

In sum then, we generally recognize that we bend the truth sometimes to avoid hurting others, but also to avoid being hurt ourselves by the reactions of others to our honesty. We are also regularly dishonest with ourselves at varying degrees of subtlety as one of the ego's major activities is to bask in its own self-generated glory.

Generosity and Compassion

These concepts are best dealt with as being closely related to each other and many people wrote of how they seem to be two sides of the same coin. Certainly in the way you wrote about them, you did raise consistent issues common to both.

Almost without exception, you all wrote of how you are very generous and compassionate with your friends and family. You argued that you were there for people close to you in times of trouble and many of the actions you outlined in the first part of the writing exemplified generous and compassionate deeds undertaken for those you love. This was often explained as a function of closeness and reciprocation—we can readily see and feel for those we relate to easily and those we are involved with in relationships that, by their very nature, involve a considerable amount of give and take. These themes were relatively easy to talk about.

Most noted though, that outside of such narrow boundaries, generosity and compassion are much less engaged. Lots of you mentioned that you really do feel compassion for those who suffer but that you do not take any practical steps to help alleviate that—by say donating money to a charity or volunteering time, or taking the initiative to act generously without being asked. Why not? The answers to this were the most interesting of all of your writing.

Some though, failed to take it further than simply noting that they don't act on internal feelings of compassion and the need to be generous. That was a lost opportunity. It was similarly a bit less than thorough to argue in the abstract about how society is all set up to deny us the opportunity to be helpful and compassionate. A large number of you took this tack and headed off into (generally sound) arguments about advertising, competition for jobs, the need to be successful materially and so forth, but most of these were distractions from the real question of why *you* don't enact these values more fully. Sure, we can point to the dynamics of the larger "system" but the deeper question would be why do we accept these constraints? And how true is it anyway (if we are brutally honest) that modern society does not give us the opportunity to be generous or compassionate? I believe that if we really think about it, we can see that there are plenty of opportunities readily available to us on a daily basis to enact these values. In some cases then, it seemed that the arguments about the external restraints were distractions from the complimentary internal restraints that more aptly account for why we do not put more of our values into action.

The more interesting and insightful papers combined observations on the structure of external reality with the dynamics of their own thinking to reveal some very interesting restraints. A few strands of this deeper thinking are worthy of discussion.

First of all, it was fascinating to note how many thought that deep down the reason for not being more generous and compassionate comes down to fear. A fair number of you wrote about how awkward you feel when someone approaches you for money or where you have the opportunity to do something helpful but where this would involve bringing attention to yourself. We all have these fears and those writing of them did a really good job of bringing these clearly to the surface. People wrote about how they wanted to volunteer (say for the City Mission) but couldn't face being there not knowing what was going on, not knowing how to interact with people whose lives are very different from our own and so forth. Others wrote about how they fear being overwhelmed if they really open up to the suffering of others and that it is so much easier to just turn one's attention away. Others spoke of the fear of being seen as "weird" or "uncool" by their friends and how rejection would be hugely painful. Others again spoke of a fear of compromising their own success if they give too much of a helping hand. And a surprising number of you made mention of how you had been treated in your own upbringing— saying effectively that you had to stand on your own two feet and received little compassion or generosity from others. Why then should you have to extend it to others? For those who wrote in this mode, you might want to ask yourself if this is really true. I think that on reflection some of you at least will be able to recognize that you had much support from others around you that was generous and compassionate.

The majority though took their thoughts in a different direction, specifically arguing that many that you could help are in fact undeserving of your generosity and compassion. I was genuinely struck by how often papers argued that the homeless or those on benefits should make more of themselves with the implication that their situation was always unenviable and always caused by their own personal failings. This was interesting because these arguments were generally quite stereotypical and I wonder how many on benefits, or how many homeless people you have talked with to get this understanding. In many cases (but not all) if we are really honest, these are nothing but prejudices and ways of relieving ourselves of responsibility.

Many of you left the reflection at that (essentially, a lot of people don't deserve my help) but the more thoughtful ones took the initiative to then ask why do I judge people in these ways? This took the enquiry into more interesting terrain. For many of these writings the answers began to reveal basic prejudices and short-cuts that we take by defining what we don't like as that which is undeserving. Questions of similarity, difference, and fear were commonly discussed in these particularly useful sections.

Finally, there were also a range of other barriers that people raised as standing in the way of more fully enacting generosity and compassion. A sense of futility was often raised along with the argument that others ought to be helping because "I am only a poor student." Many talked of the temptation to put off good intentions so that positive things can be done when you have more time, more money, more experience or a range of other factors that essentially delay the need to act now. We are not short of excuses of this nature and your answers revealed considerable insight into the dynamics that structure our mental worlds and prevent us from acting in more considerate ways. The more of these points that you integrated, the better your answer probably was.

In sum, your discussions of generosity and compassion tended to emphasize narrow boundaries of inclusion, fear of the reactions of others to being generous and compassionate, the judgments and stereotypes we use to deny responsibility and a variety of deflecting and delaying rationalizations that we all tend to use towards the ends of not compromising our own essential self-absorption.

Grades

The mark you have been given for your writing represents the extent to which you pushed yourself to deeply consider what is holding you back from being more ethical. The question is a profound one and the best answers were suitably profound. I would ask you to re-read your assignment in light of the above feedback to see how much of this richness you captured in your own account. Many people covered most of these themes and many in exceptionally clear pieces of writing. These get good grades. Many covered some of the above but stopped short of engaging the deeper questions (e.g. why do I judge in such black and white ways?) and accordingly get rewarded for good but partial explorations. A few did not go far into things at all and get lesser grades as a result. There are few comments on the papers themselves as I want to give this collective feedback but if you have any questions as to why you received the grade you did then please do not hesitate to make an appointment so that we can talk about it. I will in the meantime seek approval from some in class to share their writings with the group so that some of the particularly interesting contributions can be read by others.

We will talk about some of these themes in class as we set up the next reflective writing and take the useful things you have discovered in this exercise forward into the next line of enquiry.

Thank you all,
Ross

Feedback on Reflective Writing #2

First of all, this class deserves an acknowledgement for the generally high quality of these writings which have been among the best I have looked at for several years. The level of open engagement was very high and a number of people undertook genuinely creative and thoughtful actions that would have made a considerable number of people feel much better about their day. So well done on that front.

I mentioned in class that I wanted to give overall feedback to the group and not to write many comments on individual papers. I realize of course that this moves us into different terrain with regards to the normal expectations for feedback but I think it is a useful process. For a start it means that these writings can be returned to you within a week and I am very keen that you get prompt feedback. To write individual comments on this type of writing is very time-consuming indeed and although it can allow for a one-on-one discussion I hope that the major explanation of your grade will be covered in what follows. If it is not and you want more detailed feedback please make an appointment and I will be happy to meet and talk.

With this in mind then let me give you some feedback on your collective writing.

The range of actions you undertook was wide to say the least. People washed cars for friends, cooked dinner for flat-mates or family, took relatives shopping, to church or to lunch, helped at the City Mission, gave drinks, money or care packages to the homeless, recognized cleaners, parents and friends by giving gifts in either material or time form, some drove to give flowers to friends, baked cakes for charity, gave clothes to charity shops, donated money, guided the lost, bought petrol, drinks or bus tickets for strangers and were generous in a whole host of other ways.

1. The Nature of Action

   You were not graded directly on the nature of the action you undertook although in some cases, the sheer ambition was worthy of being recognized. In setting up the writing I emphasized the importance of pushing yourself beyond your normal habitual boundaries in order that you might open your eyes to the unexpected. Most of you clearly took that on board but quite a few completed actions that were not really far out of their normal routine. It was common in these latter writings for people to find little to say as a sister, father or friend responded as if nothing particular had happened. These gave little chance to learn anything new and accordingly, the writings were less illuminating than those where people made a genuine effort to push themselves. Points accrued to those who took the spirit of the exercise on board. These writings had an attentiveness to them that distinguished them from the ones where people didn't challenge themselves to the same extent.

2. The Quality of Reflection

   Where people entered into new actions there was much to write about and the observations were insightful. In new situations particularly, we become much more aware of our thoughts and feelings and the accounts of what you were thinking and feeling before, during and after performing the action varied a good deal. You were explicitly asked to monitor and talk about what you were thinking and feeling during these moments and those who recounted this tended to do well. However, in a number of cases people had remarkably little to say about what happened including a few instances where the action described was involved and likely to produce a very rich interaction and give lots to write about. In some instances people reported doing really big actions but wrote nothing on what the recipients did or said, and nothing on how they felt giving up considerable time, effort or money. In these cases reflection could have been much better and in a couple of extremes it was difficult to believe that the action had actually been undertaken given the almost total absence of description. Those who I really doubt have been informed on their papers and in the other instances more reflection and more direct answering of the questions posed was needed.

3. The Balance of Reflection and Theory

    A third major qualitative variation in your writing was the extent to which you wrote about the actions and reflected on these, and the extent to which broader, more abstract discussions were engaged. Many of these discussions were very good and helped provide structure and substance, but some had the balance a bit off. In some instances this meant that the vast majority of the writing was about general issues such as what a difference it would make if we were all more generous, the abstract nature of being generous in a material world and so forth. This is all potentially valuable as additional commentary but it didn't work as a substitute for the reflection on the actions undertaken. Occasionally it felt as if the action was inserted as an afterthought with the majority of the writing being on more abstract theorizing. The best ones spent most time writing about what they did and how they felt before, during and after and the impact on relationship - which was the question.

In terms of grading then, the best writings pushed for creative actions that were well conceived. These were then observed and discussed in detail to reveal a series of realizations that emerged about the self and its relationship to giving. The very good ones then tied this to broader ideas and deeper insights. If your score is above 12 (out of 15) then you did a very good job indeed. If it is less than that then hopefully you will find most of the reasons above. If you did not pass we need to talk, so please make a time to see me.

Broader Points

The purpose of this writing was to explore some of the dynamics of selfishness and the tensions that exist between self-absorption and generosity towards others. The world presents us with endless opportunities to be more generous and as such, to work on our habitual tendencies to think largely of ourselves. The first intention of this assignment was to get you looking at your daily world as an arena conducive to being generous and it was good to see so much direct discussion of this. Many people really struggled to identify where and how they might enact generosity in a way that would be challenging but not crippling. That in itself was an interesting observation. In the most uncomfortable instances people had real difficulty identifying an action and some ended up latching onto spontaneous expressions that were poorly conceived and somewhat difficult to write about.

Once actions had been decided upon there was in general, resulting admixture of excitement as the actions were planned and trepidation as people asked "But what if…" type questions. The astute among you recognized these as being self-concern in thin disguise. In such situations where we move beyond habit we do fear the reactions of others (they'll think I'm a freak, it will be embarrassing etc.) and there is a very real internal tussle between going with the immediate self-interested outcome (the relief of calling it off) and the longer-term, other-concerned outcomes. Many of you did a great job of capturing this internal dialogue and no doubt gained considerable insight into your own tendencies and capacities.

A lot of people felt very good about what they had done afterwards and many spoke of being on a high all day. For quite a few though, the expectation that this feeling would prevail was undermined in a variety of deflating ways. Some found their actions under-appreciated and a few even found that they back-fired. In many cases the primary response from the other was one of suspicion (Why are you doing this? What are you after?) These dynamics are interesting to spot and to ponder. First of all, the deflation that many felt raises the critical question of how genuine a generous act is if it demands a self-gratifying display of gratitude. It is very understandable though and one reason to show your appreciation to others' generosity at every opportunity—it keeps the motivation alive. This relates also to the feeling that many of you expressed, that you felt the recipient should respond in kind at some point in the future. Clearly a degree of self-calculation involved in such deliberations.

This no doubt relates to the observations about suspicion that so many noted. We seem to live in a world where random acts of kindness are so unusual that they seem deviant and suspicious. Many on the receiving end accordingly raised these questions directly or indirectly and very few confessed to it being a university assignment (there seemed to be a sense that this would cheapen the whole thing). Perhaps some of the suspicion of others comes from an underlying dynamic where we do feel that a gift of kindness comes with a debt of obligation attached. There are many countries in the world where this is a central principle of social exchange and where one would be rightly careful in accepting any debt- implying act of kindness from another. We however, do not live in such a tightly bound system but the implications are clearly there for some.

In conclusion then, I think that it is useful to remind ourselves of what the point of this exercise was—and that was to see what we might learn about generosity and its relationship to our own selfishness in action. Most seemed to end up with a feeling that acting in such ways is a very good thing, not only for others but also for the self. All fine and well, but the real question that follows for anyone feeling that way is to what extent are you going to continue acting in such ways in the future? Doing one act for a university assignment is easy. The real challenge to selfishness comes in doing it constantly and through breaking down the habits of selfishness slowly but surely. Being generous beyond our habits is an undertaking that is a lifelong challenge but one that many traditions would view as being the most important undertaking anyone concerned with building a better world could invoke.

Thank you then for a very good set of assignments. Hopefully this document answers some key questions regarding your mark but if you have unanswered ones please let me know. What follows are a sample of interesting and thoughtful writings and my thanks go to each writer for such helpful observations and for allowing their work to be so generously shared.

Thanks,
Ross

APPENDIX III

Sample Written and Visual Resources

The resources outlined here are from a recent course in educating *for* responsibility and give some indication of the breadth and variety of materials that can be usefully incorporated into a module of learning. This is by no means an exhaustive list of what would be on offer to learners as many other materials from the press, from TED, from You-Tube and from formal academic sources would also be added to the mix. Rather this is a set of sampled materials designed to broaden, extend and deepen perspective.

The sources below are not intended as materials for others to seam-lessly adopt as their utility depends upon the actual flow of ideas in the learning group at particular points in time and each will remain relevant for only a limited time. They do cover many on-going themes of relevance to understanding the context of modern business and each is accompanied by a brief note explaining the resource and its fit.

Most of the sources that go beyond the formal literature consist of book chapters that are contextualized as they are introduced. The visual resources that follow are drawn from on-line documentary sites where they are legitimately in the public domain and where footage is streamed rather than downloaded. Copyright restrictions in many countries limit academic courses to one chapter or a small proportion of an overall written work, and often bar academic institutions from publicly showing films to large audiences. Giving learners the opportunity to stream documentaries that are in the public domain allows access without copyright complica-tions but before using any of these sources it is advisable to check policies in one's home country and institution.

Sample Written Resources

Readings from;

Armstrong, K. (2011). *Twelve steps to a compassionate life.* London, UK: The Bodley Head.
(Well-known scholar's trenchant analysis of the centrality of compassion in all ethical systems and the means by which it can be cultivated and practiced.)

Baxter, A. (1980). *We will not cease: The autobiography of a conscientious objector.* Christchurch, New Zealand: The Caxton Press.
(Personal account of a First World War objector who was subjected to enormous punishment but still retained a pacifist stance as a moral imperative. Useful to illustrate the complexity and challenge of ethical decision making.)

Beavan, C. (2009). *No impact man: Saving the planet one family at a time.* London, UK: Piatkus.
(Interesting and often-humorous account of one person's attempt to live a completely sustainable life. Excellent contextualization of the abstract ethics of change.)

Boorstein, D. (2007). *How to change the world: Social entrepreneurs and the power of new ideas.* Oxford, UK: Oxford University Press,
(Resource for inspiring creative intervention based on the Ashoka movements support of entrepreneurs in the disadvantaged world.)

Carney, S. (2011). *The red market: On the trail of the world's organ brokers, bone thieves, blood -farmers and child traffickers.* New York, NY: Harper Collins.
(An exploration of trade in human body parts and a useful resource for testing the moral limits of markets.)

Clover, C. (2006). *The end of the line: How overfishing is changing the world and the what we eat.* London, UK: Ebury Press.
(The inspiration for the documentary of the same name that details the science of fishing, its limits and the prospects for a world with over-fished marine ecosystems.)

Csikszentmihalyi, M. (2005). *Good business: Leadership, flow and the making of meaning.* London, UK: Hodder and Stoughton.
(How values conducive to broad thriving can be implemented throughout the business process by one of the most respected psychologists working in the area of wellbeing.)

De Waal, F. (2009). *The age of empathy: Nature's lessons for a kinder society.* London, UK: Souvenir Press.
(An primatologist's exploration into the dynamics of empathy and its centrality in the social organization of primates like ourselves.)

Foley, M. (2010). *The age of absurdity: Why modern life makes it hard to be happy.* London, UK: Simon & Schuster.
(Humorous and insightful social commentary on the loss of meaning and felicity in modern marketed societies.)

Freinkel, S. (2011). *Plastic: A toxic love story.* Melbourne, Australia: Text Publishing.
(Eye-opening analysis of the role of plastic in modern life, its ubiquity, its varieties and its impacts.)

Hamilton, C. (2010). *Requiem for a species: Why we resist the truth about climate change.* Crow's Nest, New South Wales: Allen & Unwin.
(Deeply informed and no holds barred account of the future under climate change and why contemporary society finds it so difficult to change.)

Hedges, C. (2009). *Empire of illusion: The end of literacy and the triumph of the spectacle.* New York, NY: Nation Books.
(Well-analyzed accounts of cultural containment and how media shapes public attitudes and aspirations in contemporary America.)

Heffernan, M. (2011*). Willful blindness: Why we ignore the obvious at our peril.* London, UK: Simon & Schuster.
(Engaging and very well-written explorations of ethical compromise in social and business contexts. Presents a series of useful case studies and examples of the interplay of ethics and commercial activity.)

Hickman, L. (2005). *A life stripped bare: My year of trying to live ethically.* London, UK: Transworld Publishers.

(British journalist's attempt to live completely ethically for a year. Good insight into the internal struggles involved.)

Jackson, T. (2009). *Prosperity without growth: Economics for a finite planet.* London, UK: Earthscan.
(Overview of current economic and social thinking around the priority of growth and proposals for sustainable economies that can live within their physical limits.)

Jensen, D. (2010). You choose. In K. Moore & M. Nelson (Eds.), *Moral ground: Ethical action for a planet in peril,* pp. 60–64. San Antonio, Texas: Trinity University Press.
(An impassioned argument for direct action in the face of ecological decline. Good representation of more radical ecological ideas and very good for stimulating debate.)

Johnson, S. (2010). *Emergence.* London, UK: Penguin.
(A detailed scientific exploration of the patterns of emergent cooperation and the potential for harmony to reign in unplanned but highly productive ways.)

Kasser, T. (2002). *The high price of materialism.* Cambridge, MA: MIT Press.
(The well-known psychologist's account of many decades of cutting-edge research into the psychology of materialism and its social and cultural impacts.)

Leadbetter, C. (2006). *We-think.* London, UK: Profile Books.
(Social analyst considers the potential for emergence and progress under conditions of highly interconnected organizations and societies.)

Lomax, E. (1995). *The Railway Man.* London, UK: Vintage.
(A remarkable story of forgiveness from a Second World War soldier and the torturer he sought reconciliation with.)

Maass, P. (2009). *Crude world: The violent twilight of oil.* London, UK: Penguin Books.
(Detailed investigations into the "resource curse" of oil and the impacts it has on a host of national societies particularly in the underdeveloped world.)

McKibben, B. (2010). *Eaarth: Making a life on a tough new planet.* Melbourne, Australia: Black Ink Publishing.
(Founder of 350.org and one of the best explanations of the inter-relationships between human impacts and the thriving of the natural world. Excellent coverage of contemporary scientific thinking and evidence on climate change.)

Moore, K. (2010). The call to forgiveness at the end of the day. In K. Moore & M. Nelson (Eds.), *Moral ground: Ethical action for a planet in peril.* San Antonio, Texas: Trinity University Press.
(Given in partnership with the above Jensen article to represent another mode of emotional response to ecological decline and the reasons for changing business as usual). The edited book is a rich source of ethically involving writings.)

Palast, G. (2011). *Vulture's Picnic.* New York, NY: Penguin.
(Broad-ranging and award-winning investigative journalism into big oil, politics, and the public interest. Particularly good for broad perspective on the BP's Gulf Spill.)

Porritt, J. (2005). *Capitalism as if the world matters.* London, UK: Earthscan.
(A thorough analysis of what needs to change in market societies in order to further genuine social and economic progress.)

Rifkin, J. (2009). *The empathic civilization: The race to global consciousness in a world in crisis.* Cambridge, UK: Polity Press.
(Exhaustive work on the history, meaning and potential of empathy to create balance particularly in an interconnected world.)

Sandel, M. (2012). *What money can't buy: The moral limits of markets.* London, UK: Allen Lane.
(Excellent and very approachable analysis of the thin line that separates legitimate from illegitimate business and where markets need to be contained by higher principles of ethics.)

Senghe, P. (2008). *The necessary revolution: How individuals and organizations are working together to create a sustainable world.* London, UK: Nicholas Brealey Publishing.

(Examples of corporate and public interest being coordinated to good effect and a critical analysis of the need for fundamental change.)

Shaxson, N. (2011). *Treasure islands: Tax havens and the men who stole the world*. London, UK: The Bodley Head.
(Eye-opening exposé on the scale of corporate tax-evasion and avoidance and the ways by which big business keeps profits out of the public purse.)

Singer, P. (2009). *The life you can save: Acting now to end world poverty*. Melbourne, Australia: Text Publishing.
(Philosophical exploration of how we care, and fail to care for distant others and the ease with which we could make a difference. Useful for a deep analysis of the common barriers to positive compassion.)

Slater, D. (1995). *Consumer culture and modernity*. Cambridge, UK: Polity Press.
(Useful analysis of the evolution of economic thought, commodification, self-presentation and the commercial mediation of meaning.)

Steffen, A. (2010). *Worldchanging: A user's guide for the 21ˢᵗ century*. New York, NY: Abrams.
(The "Bible" of the Seattle-based Worldchanging group which is one of the most extensive collections of innovations for planetary improvement.)

Thaler, R., & Sunstein, C. (2009). *Nudge: Improving decisions about health, wealth and happiness*. London, UK: Penguin Books.
(Simple ideas on how to 'nudge' behavior towards more ethical modalities. Very good for raising not only inspiring examples but the larger dynamics of social change.)

Wilson, E.O. (2003). *The future of life*. New York, NY: Vintage Books.
(Compelling overview of the biodiversity crisis and the deeper consequences of extinguishing species.)

Woodman, C. (2011). *Unfair trade: The shocking truth behind ethical business*. London, UK: Random House.
(Investigation into a wide-range of 'Fair Trade' labels and the realities of what lies behind the labels and the labeling process.)

Young, M. (2010). *Inventing the game.* In M. Roston (Ed.), *Making a world of difference: Inspiring stories of the world's unsung heroes*, pp. 135–153. Auckland, New Zealand: Exsile Publishing.
(Creative example of doing good innovative work for the benefit of the larger community. An account of the Homeless Soccer World Cup and its growth from idea to international event.)

Yunus, W. (2007). *Creating a world without poverty: Social business and the future of capitalism.* New York, NY: Public Affairs Press.
(Account of "for benefit business" and the means by which capital and social good can be combined by creative and ethical thinking.)

Sample Visual Resources

There are many excellent documentary sites to be found on-line, several of which will send links to newly posted streaming documentaries on a daily or weekly basis. Among the most user-friendly are Top Documentary Films on Line, SNAG films, Documentary Storm and Documentary Stream. In addition, the video collections of major news channels like American Public Braodcasting, RT (Russian news channel), the BBC, Al Jazeera and many others are very well organized and easy to search. Radio and print news outlets contain equally well-archived collections covering every imaginable topic and are extremely useful for extending and deepening learners' perspectives and responding to arising issues. The list below represents the merest tip of an iceberg and readers are encouraged to browse the huge collection of available resources on the sites mentioned above.

Here are a few recent examples of films used in recent courses in educating *for* responsibility to broaden and deepen perspective. There is a quick explanation of content and use but no reference as copyright protections will differ from region to region and each is best accessed by a simple online search. The best place to begin searching though is Top Documentary Films On-Line where quality streaming is rarely an issue.

Complete Films

- **All Watched over by Machines of Loving Grace**
An Adam Curtis film about the rise of interconnection and the politics of individual and collective aspiration.

- **Blue Gold: World Water Wars**
Thorough overview of the declining availability of water and the implications for food, political and social security.

- **Catastroika**
Film looking at the debt crisis in Greece, its origins and impacts on Greek society.

- **A Class Divided**
Classic account of the roots of discrimination based on simple but powerful experiments in an American classroom.

- **A Crude Awakening**
The history, contemporary reality, and future implications of declining oil supplies and the pressures it is likely to create for business and society.

- **Cities on Speed**
Four-part documentary series on the world's mega-cities, the challenges they face and the solutions being attempted.

- **Crude**
One of the best overall accounts of climate change taking a "deep historical" approach to seeing the issue in the most fundamental terms. Highly recommended. This is an Australian Broadcasting Corporation film, not to be confused with another documentary of the same name.

- **End of the Line**
Documentary version of the book of the same name looking at the rapid decline in the world's fisheries and what needs to be done to control it.

- **Food Inc.**
Broad account of the nature of one of the most fundamental economic sectors and how it is hanging.

- **Green Gold**
  Documenting the work of Dr. John Liu who literally transforms deserts into thriving green ecosystems.

- **I am Fishead**
  Provocative film about psychopathy and its prevalence in society and business in particular.

- **Inside Job**
  The classic account of what how the financial crisis of 2007/2008 developed and played itself out.

- **Occupy Sandy**
  Useful short film on the social work being done by offshoots of the Occupy movement to rebuild community in the New York/New Jersey area following Hurricane Sandy.

- **Pray the Devil back to Hell**
  Inspiring film on the transformative power of women's resistance to armed conflict in West Africa.

- **Requiem for Detroit**
  Documentary on the changing fortunes of the Motor City as it responds to the disappearance of blue-collar work and embraces a new economy.

- **The Lightbulb Conspiracy**
  Classic film on the built-in obsolescence and the many ways in which consumption is maximized through limiting the lifespan of goods.

- **Walk to Beautiful**
  Inspiring documentary about the power of doing good. Set in Ethiopia and focusing on the transformative work of the Addis Ababa Fistula Hospital.

- **Who Killed the Electric Car?**
  Investigation into what happened in California as auto firms were forced to develop electric alternatives and then destroy them after fighting to overturn state law.

Index

OTHER TITLES IN PRINCIPLES OF RESPONSIBLE MANAGEMENT EDUCATION (PRME) COLLECTION

Oliver Laasch, Monterrey Institute of Technology, Collection Editor

- *Business Integrity in Practice: Insights from International Case Studies* by Agata Stachowicz-Stanusch and Wolfgang Amann
- *Academic Ethos Management: Building the Foundation for Integrity in Management Education* by Agata Stachowicz-Stanusch
- *Responsible Management: Understanding Human Nature, Ethics, and Sustainability* by Kemi Ogunyemi
- *Fostering Spirituality in the Workplace: A Leader's Guide to Sustainability* by Priscilla Berry

FORTHCOMING TITLES ALSO IN OUR PRME COLLECTION INCLUDE

- *Educating for Values-Driven Leadership: Giving Voice to Values Across the Curriculum* by Mary Gentile
- *Marketing to the Low-Income Consumer* by Paulo Cesar Motta
- *Managing Corporate Responsibility in Emerging Markets Issues, Cases, and Solutions* by Jenik Radon and Mahima Achuthan
- *Environmental Policy for the Business Managers* by Martin Perry
- *Teaching Anticorruption Developing a Foundation for Business Integrity* by Agata Stachowicz-Stanusch and Hans Krause Hansen
- *Teaching Ethics Across the Management Curriculum: A Handbook for Faculty* by Kemi Ogunyemi

Announcing the Business Expert Press Digital Library

Concise E-books Business Students
Need for Classroom and Research

This book can also be purchased in an e-book collection by your library as

- a one-time purchase,
- that is owned forever,
- allows for simultaneous readers,
- has no restrictions on printing, and
- can be downloaded as PDFs from within the library community.

Our digital library collections are a great solution to beat the rising cost of textbooks. e-books can be loaded into their course management systems or onto student's e-book readers.

The **Business Expert Press** digital libraries are very affordable, with no obligation to buy in future years. For more information, please visit **www.businessexpertpress.com/librarians**. To set up a trial in the United States, please contact **Adam Chesler** at *adam.chesler@ businessexpertpress.com* for all other regions, contact **Nicole Lee** at *nicole.lee@igroupnet.com*.

www.ingramcontent.com/pod-product-compliance
Lightning Source LLC
Chambersburg PA
CBHW050116210326
41519CB00015BA/3986